# FAMILY VALUES

EMPOWERED TO SUCCEED SERIES BOOK 1

# FAMILY VALUES


Dr. Carlton N. Young

*America's Grandfather*

Published in the United States of America

ISBN 978-1-962110-65-5 (SC)
ISBN 978-1-962110-64-8 (Ebook)

**Empowerment Publishing**
222 West 6th Street
Suite 400, San Pedro, CA, 90731
www.stellarliterary.com

Ordering Information and Rights Permission:

Quantity sales. Special discounts might be available on quantity purchases by corporations, associations, and others. For details, contact the publisher at the address above.

For Book Rights Adaptation and other Rights Permission.
Call us at toll-free 1-888-945-8513 or send us an email at admin@stellarliterary.com.

*This volume is dedicated to the family life we all desire to achieve for our own families. We all desire and deserve a healthy, strong | relationship for our families because strong relationships are the foundation of strong families. We need to look into our communities and our churches to help us understand what happens when a family breaks down and comes apart.*

# Contents

# Foreword

When I was first approached by Dr. Young to write the foreword for this book, my first inclination was to decline. Like many of you, I have an impossible schedule that allows me very little time for additional tasks. However, after reading the manuscript, I knew then I had to make the time in my busy schedule to write this foreword. When you read this book, you will understand why. Brace yourself!

Dr. Young is a dynamic, articulate, and heartfelt speaker, but my main reason for writing this foreword is personal. I had the opportunity to meet Dr. Young on a professional level back in 2006 when he attended my School of Motivation. After he shared his story, I was eager to get to know him on a more personal level.

From then to now, there is one word that I would use to describe Dr. Young: inspirational! For as long as I have known him, he has focused on the needs of others; his love and concern for the "American family" is unparalleled. He was a single father raising his son and daughter, teaching them old-fashioned family values, such as replying with "yes, sir" and "no, sir" and having and showing respect for their elders.

I love hearing Dr. Young talk about family conversations at dinnertime. Dr. Young teaches us how to have the hard conversations with our children, our spouses, and our parents with confidence, resulting in positive outcomes. This book is remarkable, just like its author. Don't just read the book; study it, because this man is committed to helping you rebuild, reconnect, and realize your families' dreams. This is his mission, his passion.

Dr. Young is on a mission to bring back the family values practiced by generations of the past. His book is filled with real-life experiences, information that fits situations that families currently face, and good, old-fashioned family wisdom. He designed this book to get you ready to take action in your life and make the goals and dreams for yourself and your family a reality!

No matter what your goals are in life, be they becoming a better parent, going back to school, growing your business, or overcoming obstacles, Dr. Young's wisdom as "America's Grandfather" will guide you through the different peaks and valleys toward success. This is a book I believe every reader will benefit from. You will want to purchase copies for family members, friends, and people you know who are looking to bring stability and peace back into their homes.

I highly recommend Dr. Young as a speaker, entrepreneur, father, husband, and most importantly, a human being. When I think of people that I want to associate with in my life, Dr. Carlton Young ranks at the top of my list due to his commitment to integrity. Dr. Young continues to push the envelope and challenge himself to reach new heights of achievement. Simply put, Dr. Young makes this world a better place, and I am proud to call him my friend. Dr. Young is truly the "World Champion of Inspiration!"

—Kevin Bracy
LifeChangers International
Author of *Greatness Leaves Clues* and *The Spirit of Greatness* (coming soon)

# Preface

How do we define our family values? And what are family values? Family values are the rules that parents in each household set for the growth, safety, and success of their family. They are the ideals of our grandparents and parents and hopefully other parents today who believe that living by some type of values will help keep a family committed to each other and true to the guidance, direction, and leadership styles they've chosen. What is that commitment? It's love that tells each member of their family that they are a part of something special and, most importantly, that they matter.

Today, our children have no commitment, no allegiance, and face no consequences for their actions. Today, children are able to drop out of school at ages fifteen or sixteen without their parents' consent, an age too young for them to be able to handle the hazards and hardships of adult life. These children are in no way ready to become adults, for they lack education and real-life skills. This is, in my opinion, due to the lack of family values in the home and our government's creation of unrealistic laws that give our children the upper hand and, in some cases, control over the home.

The lack of family values always leads to disrespect, irresponsibility, hard-heartedness, and miscommunication. I will discuss these values and the lack of them in *Family Values,* the first volume of a five-volume series that will explore lost family traditions. Traditions and values are the fiber that makes our families unique and brings us together. It is my opinion that we have lost our families and our children to today's generation of new technology.

I believe that every family can benefit from and be empowered by all five volumes by executing individual accountability, discipline, and passion regardless of their financial well-being. Every family member should be involved and have a valuable part in developing the family mission for their success. When our children are a part of the discussion to build and set family values, give them input. This is so important to the child.

Let's start with the definition of the word "input." It's the advice or opinions that help someone make a decision. So when you're having a discussion with your child or children, or just with family members, ask them what they would like to share, what they would like to talk about, what they are interested in, what is it they want to know, and what it means to them? Ask your child if they understand it, what they think it means, and what conclusions they may be coming to during the conversation about the situation and/or about themselves.

When we define our values, each family member will know what your family stands for and stands against, and what your family aspirations are as a whole. When our children are focused on the values we set for ourselves and our families, you will see a stronger work ethic, greater responsibility, and better communication in the household. We all must consider the long-term goals for our families, knowing that all things may not work out. Sometimes we may need to call everyone back to the dinner table and reinvasion our family plan. Come together once a quarter or as often as needed to discuss your family goals and gauge each family member's success in achieving their personal goals.

Things will change, and so will your family's circumstances. But create a family action plan and keep it out front by talking, communicating, and interacting with each other. Whether you write it down on paper or hang it on the bathroom wall, you want to ensure your family's values remain authentic and continue to reflect your own.

***

Divorce has an enormous impact on any family. Not only is it devastating to the husband and wife, it is particularly destructive to our children. Most have no idea that divorce in America has an enormous cost to Mr. and Mrs. Taxpayer each year. Through my research, I found that there is a very large group of families that demonstrate healthy family relationships, but they are overshadowed by those families who impact family and childhood development with overwhelming trauma.

When it comes to the family's decision making, allow your children to have participation in the process. But always clarify your purpose and the boundaries of your decision making: who will make the decisions, who will be affected by the decisions made, what information you need, what information is provided by your family members to help make the decisions, and when the decisions should be made. This is the foundation of any family relationship and the core of lasting and essential family values.

# Introduction

When I look at the state of our communities in regard to family models, I suspect that the American family has lost its foundation and morals. The values, principles, and standards of most of today's families have evolved into a weaker institution.

When I was growing up, our communities and families were considered to be safe and teachable places that instilled love, guidance, direction, and wisdom in preparation to succeed in the game of life. I recently had dialogue with a few single mothers, single fathers, married couples, grandparents, and adoptive parents, and collectively they all echoed the same frustration about poor parenthood examples within our communities.

How did we get to this place? Is it that the parents are getting younger and still trying to figure out life? Is it that the Internet has taken the place of family conversations and bonding? Or is it the pressures that come with trying to make ends meet to provide housing and food? All of these questions come to mind as I research this plight, but none of the answers seem to gather a precise conclusion.

When I was younger, I remember playing kickball, basketball, and even jump rope with my siblings in our backyard. We didn't have the vast technology that today's children have of being distracted with smartphones, the Internet, or cable TV. If we wanted to know something, we asked our parents for that information, or we researched in the library for clarity and knowledge. Issues about politics, dating, religion, career paths, and how to survive as a woman or man in our society were taught to us by our parents or elders in the community.

I always looked forward to Sundays because that was the time when my family would attend and participate in church. After each service, my father and grandfather would sit in the yard and discuss life, while my aunts, sisters, mother, and grandmother prepared the family dinner in the kitchen.

I was able to gather both perspectives from the yard and the kitchen about patience, guidance, and integrity.

My goal for penning this book is to discuss the state of the American family crisis and share the foundational cores of my family, which have shaped and sustained me to be the man I am today. If the glue stick of the family breaks, so does the future of our society and generations to come. Each American family must return to its heritage and take its stand as a community of refuge, education, and unconditional love.

I've learned that the key to a successful family lifestyle is practicing daily affirmations and quotes with your family. These tactics introduce the motivation and inspiration your family needs to remain robust and unified. In addition to this book, I've also written another book, *Powerful Life Quotes for Success*, which I recommend to any family in need of a resolution of change.

## Family Value #1

# The Family Dinner

*Don't be afraid of change—be afraid not to!*

—Dr. Carlton N. Young

The traditional day-to-day family dinner has changed drastically over the years, and it's no longer an exercise that unifies the family. The man of the house, the father, would use dinnertime as an opportunity to call out to God the request of protection, direction, and strength for his family. It seemed that when the family prayed together during dinnertime, they stayed together.

In today's society, families no longer sit together and have communication. Instead, children are eating microwavable meals, and teenagers are buying takeout or other fast foods. Parents used to prepare meals and talk to their children about life issues and the state of the family at the dinner table. However, these days, that picture-perfect idea is a faded reality that rarely happens.

Dr. William Doherty and Barbara Carlson, authors of *Putting Family First: Successful Strategies for Reclaiming Family Life in a Hurry-Up World,*[i] introduce the concept of the "time famine." Their research indicates that families are struggling to find the time to sit down together for dinner because they are overbooked with work, unrealistic commitments, extracurricular activities, and other contemporary worldly distractions.

Meals have become a health scare because everything these days has become a quick fix that's full of cholesterol. The obesity rate in America among children has tripled over the years due to poor food choices and the absence of parents monitoring their child's food intake. The providers of the home, whether that's single or joint parenting, work countless hours to make ends meet and to ensure their families have the necessities to function. Consequently, this new direction has invited a ball of confusion and a series of detrimental issues such as childhood obesity and child/spouse neglect, just to name a few.

Sunday afternoons were very promising when I was growing up; that was the big dinner that my family looked forward to participating in each week. Every Sunday, my grandmother would always give a stellar performance with her talent in the kitchen. She would prepare all of the ingredients and specialties over the weekend to ensure that she had everything she needed to whip up her delicate, famous dishes.

I would always look forward to eating all of my favorite foods: mixed greens, red beans and rice, corn on the cob, homemade biscuits, and my ultimate favorite, fried chicken. This food for the soul would always attract all my local family members to come together around the dinner table. There were always great conversations going on with topics about the latest community news and various events that took place within our own family.

That cherished memory is short-lived in today's society because the pride of prepping and cooking has been replaced with microwavable or prepared dinners from local restaurants. Families are no longer communicating with each other; instead, they are sitting in front of the television, surfing the Internet, or even eating in the car in rush-hour traffic.

This out-of-control behavior has garnered the attention of former First Lady Michelle Obama, who diligently fought to have this new style return back to the basics: family dinner-table time. Recently, the former first lady spoke about the values and importance of preparing and eating a meal together as a family. The former first lady Michelle Obama is an advocate for wholesome family living, and she suggests that growing your own family garden is not only creative, but essential for nutrition and wellness.

So how can the family reinstate the foundational core of family dinnertime? The answer is quite simple, and that is to stop procrastinating and schedule "family dinnertime." This simplistic method will bring the family back to the forefront of commitment and responsibility, holding each family member accountable to attend dinner.

Family dinnertime does not have to be every evening, because this obligation can be disappointing and unrealistic due to job and after-school schedules. However, if the entire family can designate a night or two each week to assemble together, then perhaps there would not be as much conflict and division among the family.

Parents can start right at their local grocery store by shopping for food together as a unit instead of alone. Such family activities can make this exercise an educational and fun experience for children. This will teach the child the importance of budgeting, and it allows the parents to enjoy quality family time by shopping for food together. Educating children on selecting fruits and vegetables versus foods high in sodium and fatty sugars can also make healthy eating rewarding and exciting.

When children are engaging in family activities as previously mentioned, the use of texting or Internet surfing should be disallowed. Fewer distractions will allow the child to stay engaged and be educated by the activity. Other good practices are to teach children how to set the table, how to have proper table manners, and how to help clean up after each meal. This structuring method will provide children with the fundamentals on how to become independent and responsible.

Naturally, most children and teenagers resist the idea of responsibility and chores, such as setting the table and cleaning up after each meal. However, once your child realizes the importance of being domestic and accountable, he or she will carry this with them into their adult life.

Great parenting is the pioneer of guaranteeing that children grow up to be well-rounded adults with morals, values, and the independence to function in the world. There are many great resources, such as parenting books and magazines, available to aid parents on how to start and handle sensitive conversations with children. Family dinnertime is an excellent time to have conversations, strengthen the family, and find out what is going on in your child's life. Say no to fast foods and microwavable dinners, and say yes to family dinnertime.

## Family Value #2

# Respecting Elders

*Wisdom is the principal thing; therefore get wisdom: and with all thy getting get understanding.*

—Proverbs 4:7, KJV

The core value of the local church is to appoint and sustain elders who work in the capacity of church mothers, deacons/ deaconesses, and ministers. These selected individuals are properly identified and qualified to showcase the true testament of faith, perseverance, and selfless service and work.

The role of an elder is to testify of God's goodness, guide the lost, set free the bound, and invite anyone who wants to change his or her life and work for God's kingdom. Through teaching and counsel, elders are able to impart the dos and don'ts of life and how to cope with struggles. Through prayer and supplication, the elders and all the counsel of the local church are able to keep the relationships between the church and the community unified.

Consequently, the presence of an elder is not always appreciated or popular because the "new-age church" does not want to do things the old-fashioned way. In other countries, the elders are held in high regard, a prestige of sorts, where respect is showcased and deserving.

The youth of today need the guidance of great counsel and wisdom so that they don't make too many mistakes that could otherwise be avoided. The elders of America built this nation. It was their blood, sweat, and tears that won wars and created the industrial giant that we are today. The trials and tribulations of the elders in America, especially minority groups, can provide valuable insight into what it means to have character and to be a positive member of a community in the face of adversity.

The youth of today would not have any of the freedoms that they exercise had it not been for someone before them securing those rights. The simplest way for young people to learn to interact with someone older is to expose them to our elderly. Our youth must become humble and learn to practice manners; however, teaching manners starts at home with the parents.

Again, parents are the child's first and most important teachers. When responding to elders, young people should be taught to make eye contact and say "yes, sir" and "no, sir." Far too many young people answer an adult with words like "yeah," "huh," "yup," or "naw," if they respond at all. These responses not only further perpetuate a lack of correct grammar and poor communication skills, but identify a lack of respect.

Demonstrating respect for an elderly person will pay off in the future when our youth one day start a family or become an elder themselves. As I previously mentioned, it all starts in the home with the parent coaching their children on how to respect and listen to the elders of the church and our community.

## The Importance of Respecting Elders

As a seasoned elder myself, I want to add that as a child, I never referred to my elders by their first name when I was growing up. I was instructed by my elders to address anyone who was older than me as "Mr." or "Mrs./Ms." For example, whenever my family would have company over or go into town to shop, it was expected of my brothers and me to open the doors, help carry groceries to the car, speak only when spoken to, and look the elder in the eye. My cooperation didn't always keep my parents and grandparents happy, but my brothers and I gave it a good try, and we were often rewarded with extra playtime or a snack afterward.

My neighborhood had many extensions of mothers and fathers who were not my natural parents, but were still given the authority to look after my brothers and me as if we were their own children. I remember an elderly lady who lived down the street from us who all the children referred to as "Big Mama." We never really knew her real name, but we were told by her to call her that.

The Bible records in Exodus 20:12 (KJV) that we should "honor thy father and thy mother: that thy days may be long upon the land which the Lord thy God giveth thee." The major emphasis of this section is to explain the importance and the role of the elder in today's society. Without their counsel, guidance, and wisdom, our nation and communities will suffer tremendously.

We stand on the shoulders of the greatness of our elders who have been around longer and are wise enough to protect us from what is ahead in our future if we are not careful. We all must commit to taking the time to listen to what they have to say and hold our children accountable for their lack of respect. My father would often say to my brothers and me, "If you want to know real world history, ask your grandpa. He's a pillar of knowledge!" My grandpa was one of the most brilliant men I knew other than my father, and it seemed that he always knew the answers to all of my questions.

My wife's grandmother is still alive today, and she recently turned one hundred years young and lives with us. My wife and I have become very patient with her because she can sometimes move too slowly and can't remember too much. But through all of her health and memory issues, we still look at her as an elder who has conquered life and the test of time through her faith in God.

**NOTE: For more information on services provided for people over fifty, visit www.aarp.org.**

## Family Value #3

# The Family That Prays Together Grows Together

*"After this manner therefore pray ye: Our father which art in heaven, hallowed be thy name, thy kingdom come, thy will be done in earth, as it is in heaven. Give us this day our daily bread. And forgive us our debts, as we forgive our debtors. And lead us not into temptation, but deliver us from evil: For thine is the kingdom, and the power, and the glory, for ever. Amen."*

— Mathew 6:9-13 (KJV)

The Lord's Prayer is the first prayer my parents taught us when we were growing up, and I later taught it to my own children and grandchildren. I found this great prayer to be the solution that covers everything I need from God in times of trouble and when I need direction in life. It was prayers like the Lord's Prayer that I would recite when I was in school. However, prayer has been taken out of the mainstream of schooling along with the Pledge of Allegiance.

I suspect that the reason for today's students bullying each other in the classroom, killing one another, threatening their teachers, having sex, and using profanity as a second language is because prayer has been taken out of the school system. I'm a firm believer that prayer really does change things, and it's very necessary in our homes and schools. Prayer was taken out of the public school system when the United States Supreme Court issued two bans, one in 1962, the other in 1963. Both bans were results of lawsuits against practicing religious practices by faculty and staff in schools.

In 1963, ant-prayer groups were organized to petition against the use of any form of prayer or reference to God in schools. These organized groups argued that prayer was a violation of the separation of church and state, and schools that were publicly funded were an extension of the state.

The lawsuit was supported by dozens of organizations, but through my research I discovered that Madalyn Murray O'Hair, the founder of the American Atheists (a nationwide nonprofit organization that defends the civil rights of nonbelievers), was the biggest supporter of this catastrophic movement.

As I played back the turn of events in my head, I suddenly remembered my grandmother saying these words: "*If they take prayer and God out of the school, in time the devil will come to class.*" My grandmother was very wise with her prediction, because that is exactly what has happened. They took God and prayer out of the classroom, and the devil's been there ever since.

The Pledge of Allegiance was viewed as a forced religious practice that was inappropriate and not socially acceptable. As I researched this, I was able to gain clarity on what the Pledge of Allegiance really meant, and how important it is in our school systems. "Allegiance" means your loyalty to that which you have made a pledge to protect. The word "pledge" means a promise to take responsibility for your actions, such as your family, home, marriage, school, work, or country.

Today, young people don't have anything to pledge to or have pride in anymore. Back in my day, the biggest worry we had as students in school was someone taking your lunch or pushing you out of line so he or she could be first. We as a nation have lost our power, our classrooms, and if we're not careful, we also may lose the opportunity to give our children positive influences. I believe that if families would bring prayer back into the home and back into America's schools, it would make a huge difference in the lives of our children.

I also stand firm on my opinion that ever since prayer was removed from our school systems, technology and music videos have negatively captured the attention of our children. I researched premarital sex and teen pregnancy in young teenage girls ages fifteen and nineteen years old; according to City-Data.com, teen pregnancy rates were less than 15 percent per thousand before 1963. After 1963, when prayer was taken out of our schools, teenage pregnancies increased by an all-time high of 187 percent.[ii]

The article also stated that fifteen years later, for younger girls ages ten to fourteen, pregnancies since 1963 are up 553 percent. Before 1963, sexually transmitted diseases among students were four hundred per one hundred thousand. Since 1963, they are up 226 percent.

It's my opinion that removing prayer from our schools is not recognizing prayer in the home or in our children, who no longer have anything or any reason to have an allegiance with or make a pledge to. When I look back over my journey through life and becoming a single parent, I realize that over the years, single motherhood, once limited only to poor women and minorities, is now becoming the new way of life, "the norm." When there is no man in the home within the African American community, 72 percent of households are then headed by single mothers.[iii] So in many of our communities today, 72 percent of America's households don't even know what it's like to have a father in the home on a day-to-day basis.

What that is saying to me is there is no allegiance to home, family, God, and country. When I joined the United States Marine Corps years ago, the men and women all made a pledge to serve God and country. It's my opinion that the American family is in a downward spiral. Even though it's the twenty-first century, we still have a large racial divide across America.

Many young people don't have relationships with any positive male role models, and they are raising themselves and learning about life from their peers and/or from a single female (not that this is a bad thing). But without a positive male role model for a young man to follow after, many grow up not knowing what it really takes be a responsible man/father and a great provider for their families.

There are many myths and commissions put on young black men today, and these myths and commissioned studies show why more young black males are in prison than in college. According to the American press, these myths are untrue. In a 2013 column for *The Root*, Howard University professor and Congressional Black Caucus Foundation analyst Ivory A. Toldson said: "The myth about there being more black men in prison than in college is the most frequently quoted statistic about black men in the United States."[iv] An article in the February 12, 2013, edition of *Vox* talked about the myth's source, its impact on communities of color, and evidence that clearly proves the myth's fallacy.[v] According to the United States census, about 18,508,926 in the US population are black males of all ages.

In 2013, 1,437,363 were enrolled in college, according to the National Center for Educational Statistics.[iv]

I would like to focus on a subject that explains why our young black men in America are considered to be an endangered species. The issues on the plight of the black male in America can no longer be ignored. The time to address these issues is overdue. When we look at the problems that take place in white communities, they don't compare with the problems that occur in our black communities.

There is a large percentage of young black children in our communities that is fatherless and living in a single-parent home. Growing up in this type of community, I can say that there is a large number of young black children born out of wedlock or living in a single-parent home being raised by their mothers. An article by National Religious Broadcasters (NRB) states that the pregnancy rate among black females is higher than any other race. Gail Taylor, a research columnist for the NRB magazine, tells us in her research that "black males between the ages of fifteen and twenty-four share an unusually high risk of dying from black-on-black crimes."[vi] This has been a long-standing issue for years, and not much has changed. The statistics have become factual and they are all still the same. And yet, young black males are still the most feared group in America."

While young black females without a positive male role model also deal with the same issues of fear, they are not being raised to respect their bodies. They want to be grown and think they know everything. They fight like males, and they are some of the most disrespectful students in school. They dress like adult women, and they feel that they know more than what can be told to them. They learn about sex and boys from watching TV. They want to be sexy before their time, and many want to have a baby because they think it's popular.

America's youth is in big trouble, and I feel it's because there aren't any positive males at home to enlighten them on how to enjoy being children, and how to grow up to be positive adults.

I have to be real with you on this subject and tell you that I grew up with my dad and mom in the house. Now my dad worked away from the home; his job took him away from home for months at a time, and sometimes he would be gone for about a year. So my mother became Mama and Daddy to both me and my siblings. I know now that it can be very stressful at times, but as a child I had no idea what stress was or what it could do to a person.

Now I can see that being a single parent, whether that means you are divorced, single, or separated, brings many challenges to the home, and everyone is affected. I understand that being a single parent puts demands on you, your time, and your children, but saying nothing about the energy it takes to be a single parent can add even more stress. How would you know about the stress of being a single parent? That's the question you might be asking yourself!

Well, if you must know, I was a single father raising my son and daughter alone, at times with no assistance from friends and family. After about two years, my daughter left to go live with her mother, but my son stayed with me. To make a long story short, my son and I ended up on the streets as a homeless family. For more than three years, I raised my son out of the trunk of my car with no shelter and no place for us to go.

This could have been tougher on women who find themselves in the unfortunate situation I was in with my son. When there's no man in the home, women have to handle more responsibilities alone. But you are not by yourself, because there are millions of single mothers out there who you can lean on and depend on to help you make it through the hard times.

One thing I did that you might want to look into doing yourself was going to classes to learn about being a single parent. I did this on my own. The class was all women and I was the only male, but I learned so much; we all did by coming together and sharing our personal stories. By doing this, your experience and the experiences of other single parents will give you the chance to develop your self-confidence, make new friendships, and develop new relationships with other single parents. Now here's the kicker: being a single parent is no picnic. It's not easy at first, but I'm sure you already know that.

Here's what I think the problem is when there is no man in the home. I found myself doing this very same thing. You aren't the "father," you're the "mother"—so be one! Stop worrying about the father not being home and start looking at how much better you can be as a mother, provider, and most importantly as a teacher to your child. Let your children understand the importance of who they are, where they come from, and the greatness that is in their futures. It's going to take you and you alone to make the changes in your new single household for the positive outcome, but do the best job you can for the future and well-being of your children.

## Balancing Work and Family

I found that being a single parent can bring on some feelings of guilt, grief, and at times, loneliness. You can overcome these feelings once you learn to bring balance back into your life. One way to bring balance back into your home and work is that if your child or children are old enough to come home from school and stay home alone, you can make sure they understand your rules, not what they may think should take place, such as having friends over without permission, leaving the house without permission, or using the telephone instead of doing homework or chores. One of my biggest points I made very clear to my son (you should make it clear to your children) is how to reach me when I am still at work if there is an emergency.

Moms, remember this one thing if you don't remember anything else: you are NOT your child's best friend. You're their parent, and they do what you say to do at the time you say to do it. As a single female in the home with no man present, you are "top dog." You run things, and you cannot let your child see you sweat. Your time to cry is at night in your bedroom if you need to release your frustration. Don't feel sorry for yourself; I tell you to cry so you can release your anger.

I'm six foot one, two hundred thirty pounds, and a retired marine. But there were times when I would lie in my bed, or the times my son and I slept in the car, and I would cry. But the next day, I got up, washed my face, and went out to face the world head on. No more excuses because you don't have a man around. It's always good to be a complete family, but it's not always the case. You don't need a man to validate who you are, because you are strong with or without him.

## No Means of Support

Not having a man or not knowing what to do without one is not a valid excuse. Life is like dining at a smorgasbord restaurant—there is something for everybody in the end. It's all about you staying focused and knowing you're not alone. When the storms of life beat you down and you're now in that place called “no means of support,” that’s the time you have to reach down and grab ahold of life and understand the season you’re in.

Make no excuses for what goes wrong, and never apologize for your success. Strengthen your relationships with other single parents, your family, and, most of all, with the people closest to you, like friends and neighbors. You have all the support you need next door, down the street, and within your entire community. Stop thinking you don’t have any support, stop feeling sorry for yourself, and stop apologizing for what you don’t have. You have every resource you need, but you have to reach out for help.

## Family Value #4

# Mothers Who Are Both Mom and Dad

I recently read a book written by a single father who wrote about not only being a single dad to his kids, but filling in for the role of mom, too, at times. In his book, he talks about how single mothers should deal with issues that only a dad should have to handle. He discussed the conversation he had with a single mother who found it difficult to talk to her teenage son about sex and how to become a man. He writes that it is hard for a mother to also be a dad, but it's done every day in millions of households.

As a grandfather, my message to these mothers is if you are raising a young boy to become a man, stop comparing him to his father. I was at a local mall a while back in Atlanta, Georgia, for some holiday shopping and I overheard a single mother reprimanding her son. I was shocked to hear her say to him, "You're just like your no-good daddy! Straighten up, boy!" Her comments got me very upset because she should have not said that to him at all, especially not in public, if you ask me.

This type of behavior causes conflict between the mother and the son, and soon he will start to lose respect for his mother. Let's talk about when a woman brings a child into the world and he or she takes their first breath of life. The journey for both mother and child begins at that moment. A mother's love is the most powerful force on the planet, and a woman will do anything that she has to do to provide for her children, and for that she should be praised.

I think we as parents may forget that our children are not born with that sense of self-respect. We are in charge of teaching our children to respect their parents, teachers, and others. Our children, yours and mine, have very different personalities and need to be taught to be respectful.

I want to dive a little deeper into the current state of our young men in America by talking more about single parents who happen to be mothers.

Let's imagine for a minute a typical day in the life of a young man who is being raised by a single mother. He lives with his mom; when he goes to school he is most likely taught by a female teacher, and then comes back home to Mom. Unless he is in a sport where there are other young men, or he has uncles and other male family members who are active in his life, this young man will become overly stimulated with female traits.

Consequently, as a teenager he will begin to seek out male role models on his own to help him find his way in the world, but at that point we just might lose our young men to the streets. As strong as a mother's love is, it sometimes is no match for the excitement out there on the streets. In the outside world, a young man sets his own limits, he follows his own rules, and he thinks he's free to be the man that he always wanted to be.

There are so many single mothers who have the responsibility of doing everything in the house, from problem solving to buying the groceries, cooking meals, washing and folding the clothes, overseeing homework assignments, planning birthday parties . . . The list just goes on and on. To eliminate some of these problems, the single mother can enlist the support of men at an early age for her son to be around. If she has no extended family, she has to be strategic about enrolling her son in programs that are staffed by men who care about molding young boys into young men. Local nonprofits such as Boys and Girls Clubs, karate, boxing, or apprentice programs can help your son gain what he needs for manhood.

There are many celebrities who focus on our young men, with organizations such as the Steve Harvey Foundation, the Carmelo Anthony Foundation, NFL camps, NBA Cares, and Dr. Steve Perry's Save My Son program. There are several competitive academic summer programs operated by local and state government dollars that give our young men a chance to work as interns. The one thing that is for sure in America is that opportunities are endless when you ask for assistance as a single parent.

If you live in a community where there is a lack of positive outlets for your son to participate in, then it's time to make some noise and demand more from your city and local leaders. Collaborate with teachers and the school board to find out how the lives of the youth can be enriched. This is something I have seen very little coming from parents both married and single. If you can't get answers there, attend a city hall meeting or contact your mayor's office to shake things up a bit. Write your elected officials and make your child a part of the process.

Single mothers try their very best to give their children as much guidance and provisions as they possibly can, but let's remember that as a female, there are just some things a single mother can't give to her children. I say this because I remember as a single father there were times when I was unable to give my children motherly advice, because I was their father.

For example, a single mother is unable to explain or set an example for her children in the areas of confidence, praise, and attention that only fathers can give their daughters and sons, in my opinion. When it comes to young boys, the single mother can't give a young man the father-son relationship that he needs and cherishes during his golden years as he develops into manhood.

Today's mothers are becoming younger and younger, and that is also a huge issue for young, single mothers because they don't have the wisdom to be a mother, let alone to become both mom and dad to their children. A large number of our young, single mothers are trying to raise their children alone, but they are inexperienced and scared. Raising a child alone is not an easy task for a young man or young woman, especially when they are between the ages of sixteen and eighteen. At this age, there is no way that they are able to successfully provide their children with emotional and financial support.

For a single mother, motherhood is like two sides of a coin—while you have the joys and the bliss of being around your child, you also have the difficulties and the stress associated with it.

Being a single mother is probably the most difficult part of single parenting. Whether a woman is a single mom by choice or because of getting divorced, it is very hard to play the role of both parents. Remember, a child needs the love, care, concern, attention, and adoration of both parents.

The absence of the presence and influence of a male role model in a child's life, if not careful, can be detrimental. Becoming a single parent does not make you less lovable; it just means that you have more responsibilities than before. All you need to do is be strong and learn to face the harsh realities of life with strength and endurance.

## Mom and the Household

When you are the single mom and find yourself left to operate the household alone, the first thing I recommend for you to do is get yourself organized. It's now about the well-being of you and your children, and if you think your back is against the wall, that's only because you backed up, and as long as you stay there, the pressure will grow and come at you from all angles. My advice to you as a single mom is to prioritize your time and ensure that you're organized and balanced.

Balance is good to have between your home and job, and you should never let the two worlds cross each other. When you're at work, you're at work; when you're at home, you're at home. Single mothers should make sure that they are doing their best job at work so the bills can stay paid, and when they come home, they should devote that time to nurturing their children.

## When Trouble Comes Home

Every day, families have to deal with issues that shake their foundation, such as being unemployed. Many families are living from paycheck to paycheck, trying to keep a place to live, food, and enough money stacked away for emergencies. Many families are trying to save money so that they can send their children to college one day, so that student loans and other expenses will not be that difficult for their children.

The courts have taken children away from homes when the family can no longer provide a safe environment for them and when the "system" stops working to provide the help that is needed. These are hard times for the American household, but trouble doesn't always last. I believe that even in the toughest of times there is always a way out. I know that prayer, faith, and knowing how to solve problems can bring hope in troubled times. "Seek and ye shall find" (Matthew 7:7, KJV) is a common phrase among churchgoers in times of confusion and turmoil.

## What to Consider When Trouble Comes

When trouble comes, we need to consider the reasons why those troubles are coming to us. Please! Stop fooling yourself when you know the real reasons that need to be dealt with. It's too often that when we face trouble in our lives we play the blame game, or act as though we don't know why these things are going on in our lives. I read a saying some years ago that stated, "Happiness is based upon the happiness in my life, but joy comes from the Lord."

What this statement means is that trouble in our lives is caused by the emotions we are unable to control when we are upset. Anger, depression, fear, grief, and rejection are what trouble feeds on. When trouble takes over in an area of our lives, we try to work it out on our own because, at the time, it seems easy. I believe what we are missing during times like these is spiritual growth. We need not only develop a relationship with God for ourselves, but also for the development of our personal and family growth. I personally believe that when troubles come, it's a test of our faith.

When I lost everything, and I found myself living homeless on the streets, there was a part of me that gave up, and that part of me opened the door for more trouble and spiritual warfare in my life. Let's face it: most of us are not spiritually ready to fight that fight. Don't get angry—you know it's true! I found myself down and out on the streets of Atlanta, Georgia, and as a homeless man for a little more than three years, I became very angry. My emotions—anger, depression, fear, grief, and the feeling of rejection—all weighed on me heavily as I tried to understand what was going on in my life.

But here's the kicker: after being down for three years, I realized the only person who was keeping me down was me. I allowed the trouble in my life to control my emotions, which made me remain in my homeless situation longer than I should have. You see, when trouble comes into your home, you have the option to either invite it in or dismiss it from your life.

Many unexpected things take place in our lives that can bring great trouble to our doors—things like when your car is repossessed or you lose a job or even a loved one. But if we know how to handle our emotions, we can handle the trouble that stands at the door. We often allow trouble to follow us home, and we invite it in. I'm talking about allowing it into our hearts and minds. You can't function or think clearly, so you react out of fear and anger, which later lead to a state of depression and rejection. But the truth of the matter is you don't have to go through it.

## Trouble and the Journey In-Between

*The power of your words and the power of your vision will create the power in your life.*

—Dr. Carlton N. Young

One of my great friends, Helen Carter-Johnson, author of *Golden Memories of Childhood* and *When There Is No Visual Means of Support*, talked to me about the prisons of life and what category we may find ourselves in based on our circumstances. Helen asserted that trouble can weigh heavily in the mental or physical areas, and sometimes both can affect our lives. I'd venture to say that our prison is the emotional state that we allow our troubles to keep us in. There are times when certain things in our lives need to be worked out before they create the trouble we don't want or need.

There was a time in my life when I lost a great-paying job I had held for five-plus years, and immediately after losing that job, I fell into a state of deep depression. This unexpected and tragic period in my life allowed trouble to come into my life that I didn't need to experience. Everything you go through in life is a test, and when trouble comes before you, try and learn from that test.

I met a young mother who worked at a grocery store as a cashier and had two small children to raise on her own. Based on her income, she was eligible to qualify for medical coverage and food stamps. The state social-services program is set up in such a way that if she were to earn over a certain amount per month, she would have to report it, and then her benefits would be in danger of being reduced or taken away for good. In addition, she also wanted to go to college, but she wasn't sure how she would pay for it. She continued to pray about it, and in her dreams she could see herself in a classroom learning and one day graduating.

Brushing off her dream as a mere wish, the young lady continued to work at the grocery store until both of her children were school age. However, she still struggled, and eventually her lights were cut off for nonpayment, among other bills she was past due on. There were also times when she didn't have enough money to take the bus to work, or for the babysitter to keep her sick child, so she had to call off from work often.

Again, God gave her a desire to go to college, and this time she listened. The young lady quit her job and applied to attend college. Not only did she get grants and loans to cover the cost of tuition, she was able to use the extra money to pay for her living expenses. After two years in college, she applied for an administrative assistant job with the college that she attended.

Her previous experience in customer service at the grocery store was the perfect training, and she landed the position. All of a sudden, her tuition was half price and she no longer needed the loans to live off of. She enrolled her children in an after-school program, took classes right after work, and graduated with a four-year degree at the top of her class.

## The Rules of Engagement

When you see trouble coming to your home, first take stock of your life and reflect. You should think about the job that you are working and the right time you should look for opportunities to advance. Can your skills be transferred to another setting? Are you educated enough? If not, consider gaining some additional training either through an internship, coursework, or an apprenticeship.

Have you reached out to all of the local and state agencies that offer assistance? Have you called on family and friends? What about prayer? What are the desires of your heart? What dreams do you have at night? If you are experiencing debt or financial difficulty, contact your creditors to make payment arrangements that you can stick to, even if it's just ten dollars per month. The key to overcoming life's challenges is to make up your mind to make the change for the better and take action to make it happen.

## Dealing with Youth Who Are Out of Control

I can remember when I talked back to my mom, acting like I was "grown," and my mom was not going to let me be grown. She said to me, "Boy, go outside, get the biggest switch that you can find, and bring it to me." She wanted me to get the switch that she was going to use to beat my butt.

I can also remember when my cousin got in trouble and how my dad beat him with a belt, or when my best friend talked back to one of the neighbors and his dad beat him all the way home with an extension cord. Yes, an extension cord. Don't act like you've never heard of that before. He cried and screamed like he was being killed all the way home. I took off running and left my friend to his fate. Some best friend I am, you think.

These were the ways that young people in my day were put back in line, and it kept most of us out of jail. We were too afraid to talk back or deal with our parents who didn't play that and would beat our butts to beat some "sense" into us. And trust me, it worked.

Let me start with this: when I was growing up, our parents didn't play that bull! Now some of us feel that we have tried just about everything we know to get a handle on our out-of-control children, but we all have the same questions on what we should do and how we should it. How do I stop the acting out at home, school, and in public? How do we stop the arguments? How can I get my teen to follow our rules? These are many popular questions that parents may have when disciplining their children.

I can remember talking back to my mother. We're talking early to late '60s, when the neighbors could help make that midcourse correction on your butt, drag you home, and throw you into your house, and your parents would never ask them any questions. They would just pick up where the neighbor left off. I can remember talking back to my mother, but Mama was not having that, so she would slap me in the face. Most of the time, my older brother would volunteer his services to either go out and get the switch, or he would offer to help hold me down so my mother could beat my butt.

I can recall acting up in elementary school in the sixth grade and how Mama came into my classroom and beat my behind with a belt in front of the entire class. Just a little word to the wise: when your mother is the playground monitor, remember to keep a low profile. My mother even came and got me out of classes in high school and took me home and beat my butt, and then she took me back to school. I was in the eleventh grade at that time.

The thing of it is we lived through it. Although at the time we may have thought differently, it made us better men and women today. These were some of the ways that young people back in my day were disciplined.

Most of today's parents are frustrated and at the end of their ropes, but it's not just the parents; defiance is a common behavior in our youth today.

Consequently, things can be worse, and we all have seen that in some of today's youth. Today, the hands of the parents are tied. Back in my day, all it took was a look from Dad and my grandmother saying to my cousin and me, "If you don't start acting like you got some good sense, I'm going to beat some sense into you." And trust me, it worked.

## Choose Your Battles

I read an article by Barbara Solomon of *Parents Magazine*. The article read:

> *Many parents who've been enjoying their pleasant, cooperative third- and fourth-graders think that they have a few more years of smooth sailing before the challenges of raising teenagers set in. But experts say it's often during the middle-school years that kids begin acting out. As they straddle the fence between childhood and adolescence, they can become secretive, moody, and defiant. "Preteens are starting to assert their independence, and that can create tension between them and their parents," says John Davis, author of* Don't Take It Personally: A Parent's Guide to Surviving Adolescence.[vii]

My grandmother used to say that when dealing with out-of-control children, "A part of their nature is misbehaving and acting out. It's all in their growing process." And she would look over at me and say, "You, for one, should know that. You were the worst of the bunch." As I said earlier in the book, take prayer out of school and all you have left is hell. I'm old school and I still believe in spare the rod, spoil the child.

My brothers and I, along with my cousin, were the bad boys of our neighborhood, but we never broke into anyone's house, never stole any cars, and we never carried a gun. Our biggest crime spree was stealing watermelons from Old Man Murphy's garden. We would run into the drive-in movie and turn up two to three microphones, run back out, and sit on the fence and watch the movie. The difference is this: Back in my day, we knew how far we could go, but today's youth go too far.

Let me be very clear and say I'm not advocating child abuse—not at all. I don't think a child should be disciplined every single time he or she does or says something wrong. We all make mistakes; that's part of our learning process and it's what makes us human. Keeping the lines of communication open with your children, establishing rules and routines in your household, and assigning kids chores and making them responsible for their space are all positive parenting techniques that work well with most children. Talking to your child about your expectations and living your life in a way that provides a real example of how they should conduct themselves in society are sure ways to nurture your child.

But what happens when you've tried all of the above and your child is still causing you trouble? I can tell you how I made it work for me, and I hope that what I did will be helpful to you to understand how to deal with your youth as a single parent. After I retired from the Marine Corps, I was living in Deal City, Virginia, and I worked in Washington, DC, as a single parent living with my daughter and my son. I would commute back and forth on the bus. It was during this time that I realized the most important question you should ask yourself as a parent.

## Who Is Your Child Hanging out With?

My daughter became friends with a young girl across the way from where we lived. I used to hear this young lady talk to her father in such a rude and disturbing manner that I told my daughter I didn't want her hanging around her—and I meant that.

Let's cut to the chase. Over time, my daughter became as rude as this young lady, to the point that she quit school at age fifteen and told me that there was nothing I could do about it. And she was right. I took off work and went to the school to see how this could even take place without my consent. That's when I was told by the school principal that the State of Virginia has a law that a child can quit school at the age of fifteen without the parents' consent, and there is nothing the parents can do or say about it.

I was told that I was still responsible for her actions even though the State gave her the right to make her own choice about school and her education. I believe my daughter got her rude and nasty ways from this young lady. I'm not saying my daughter was the angel that fell from grace, but I could see some trouble coming a long way off. This young lady just helped to jump-start my daughter a little earlier.

*Show me your friends and I'll show you your future.*

— John Kuebler

We all are influenced by someone or something at some time in our lives. What is it that we are showing our children? This is a question we must ask ourselves, and we need to be aware of what and who our children are being influenced by from outside the home.

## Consequences

*Honor thy father and thy mother; that thy days may be long upon the land which the Lord thy God giveth thee.*

—Exodus 20:12, WBT

The youth of today have no fear of the law, but what's worse is they have no respect or honor for their parents. We didn't go to church that much as children growing up, but I do remember my grandmother saying that if we didn't obey our parents, we would not live long on the earth. One thing I have come to notice is that a lot of youth today don't care about the consequences.

I remember the time I had to work a long weekend on my job one Sunday night. Whenever I worked weekends, I would drive into DC, and this particular Sunday night, my daughter called me and asked if she could go to the movies. I told her no because I did not want her to leave her younger brother home alone. Plus, it was a school night.

After I thought about my daughter wanting to hang out, I remembered that the mall was closed on Sunday nights by 7:00 p.m., so I knew something wasn't right. I drove home to find her gone and my son home alone. I put my son in the car and we drove to the mall. It was close to closing time, so I knew that there were no movie theaters open.

I sat down in the mall and eventually my daughter walked by with three young men. When I called out her name, I could see the surprise in her eyes when she saw me. I'm sure she could hear the anger in my voice when I said, "Let's go! It's time to go home!"

My daughter turned to face me and replied, "I'm not going anywhere with you and you can't make me, so *fuck you*!" When she said that, the three young men made a circle around me as if they were going to jump me, and to my astonishment, my daughter said to me, "I will help my friends kick your fucking ass."

When I didn't back down, I think the young men got the message from the look on my face: I was going to be the last one to hurt that night. But I knew that if I got into a confrontation with them, I would be the one going to jail. My daughter made a statement that hurt me badly. She continued to tell me she wouldn't be coming home at all that night.

Three days passed and I hadn't seen her, but when she finally did show up, I told her she needed to go stay with her friend across the way because I was not having that kind of conduct under my roof. We got into a heated argument and she used the most profane language you can imagine, so I slapped her in the mouth. She bit her lip and started to bleed. It was nothing to be alarmed about, but she made a big production out of it. She ran out of the house and across the way to her friend's house.

If you have a child who doesn't seem to understand consequences and is taking advantage of you and your patience, you may have to put your child in his or her place by removing extracurricular activities or items that he or she enjoys, such as video games, television, cell phones, etc. If your child continues to push the limits and begins to curse you out, run away from home, or even become violent with you, then you have to take drastic measures and establish yourself as the parent by using the belt and whipping that ass.

Now I know what the law says, but we all know what the Bible says as well. I'm not talking child abuse; I'm not telling you to go against the law, but I know what the word of God says. Today we have lost our children to the streets because the law has taken our right to discipline our children. Children these days threaten their parents with the police and use the system against their parents to get their own way.

Not long ago, a young man here in Atlanta shot his mother eight times because she wouldn't give him her credit card. My own daughter called the police on me for hitting her, but when the police arrived and saw how rude she was and how nasty her mouth was, they didn't blame me for striking her and acknowledged that she was out of control.

Discipline is a part of raising children, and if you punish your children early and train them in the right way by demanding respect and establishing boundaries, they will know that there will be consequences for their actions of disobedience. One thing is for sure: if you set goals with objectives that are attainable for your child, they will give you fewer problems down the road. Ignoring a child's disrespectful ways when they are young gives them fuel to act recklessly when they are older. I'd rather slap my daughter in the mouth for talking crazy to me and raising her voice than have her walk around thinking it's okay to speak to me or any other adult that way. There is danger in not disciplining your child.

Society doesn't care who your child is. If your child conducts themselves with ignorance toward others, then they will be treated accordingly. Again, I would rather go to jail for whipping my child than go to their funeral. As a grandfather, if I don't show my granddaughters how to interact with young males, then I am setting them up to be less than a lady when they get into the world and start dating.

If my granddaughters think it's okay to yell and curse at me, then they will think that it's okay to do the same to their boyfriends or husbands. But unlike me, their boyfriends or husbands may not be able to control themselves and may hurt my granddaughters or worse because of their smart mouths. For mothers raising teenage sons who are out of control, I don't advise that you try to physically challenge your son. I would rather you partner with male mentors or enlist the help of the child's father or uncle to work with him.

Any male child that hits his mother isn't healthy and should be handled by a man or a professional therapist. For mothers raising out-of-control teenage girls, get a counselor involved. Maybe your teen is suffering from a mental illness such as depression and requires professional support. The most important thing is to keep a notebook on incidents involving the disciplining and the actions of your child, because if a child becomes angry and makes a false statement about you to the authorities, you could find yourself in trouble with the law.

If you have a written record of the times when your child was out of control and the strategies that you tried before you disciplined your child, then you are in a better position to defend your actions. Troubled children can sometimes do irrational things, and once the call to the police or social services has been made, you have to prove that you are doing what's in the best interest of your child.

## Family Value #5

# It Takes a Village to Raise a Child (A Message to Fathers)

*What defines a father? Merriam-Webster defines father as "a man who has begotten a child; a sire; a leading man; one that originates or institutes."*[viii]

Traditionally, fathers act in a protective, supportive, and responsible way toward their children. Involved fathers offer specific provisions to their sons and daughters throughout their life cycle. Active fathers play a role in reducing negative behavior and psychological problems in young men and women. In fact, a rise in the amount of father-child interactions will help increase a child's social stability, educational achievement, and their potential to build strong relationships as an adult.

Children are curious about the world and need positive adults to model problem-solving skills. When children don't have involved fathers, they seem to ignore the obvious by not following through on your rules and the consequences. Our children need to have a positive male in their lives to teach them about the world and the meaning of life. A father doesn't always have to be the child's biological parent. Many children live in homes with a stepfather, uncle, or a grandfather. In fact, stepparents and extended family members have an important role to play in raising children.

Studies suggest that high rates of divorce contribute to a substantial proportion of American children being raised in stepfamilies.[ix] Forty percent of married couples with children (i.e., families) in the United States are step partners wherein at least one partner has a child from a previous relationship.[x] As a father of three (one of which is a stepson, but more on that in the second volume), it takes more than making a baby to be called a father. Being a father requires time, attention, support, love, commitment, and lots of prayer. I have met too many young, middle-aged, and older men who talk about their children but are not involved fathers. They help in the production of making the child, but once the child gets here, they leave.

These types of men cannot be called fathers because a real man, a real father, would never do anything like that.

## A Message to Men Who Are Real Fathers: Will the Real Men Please Stand Up?

My favorite part of doing business is traveling. I enjoy having conferences with the men and speaking to them about our roles as fathers and leaders in the home. I need you to keep an open mind as you read this message: Fatherhood is a responsibility created by God, and it should be taken seriously. Women carry, deliver, and nurture children, and they work inside and outside of the home raising children alone when men don't step up to the plate.

Ultimately the seed is planted by a man, and because of this, a father must continue to sow wisdom and love into the life of that child in order to lay the foundation for proper growth. The father's involvement in their child's life is essential to that child's growth and development. Men and women are different; they think differently and act differently. We all have our own opinions about single moms becoming the heads of the household. The sexual revolution of the sixties, women's liberation, and the mobility of families has added to role reversal, and women are taking on leadership positions in society and in the home.

As consumers in America, we have become accustomed to replacing things and people. Need a new house? Move. Need a new car? Buy one. Need a new spouse? Get a divorce, leave, and find a new one. People no longer have to remain in relationships where they think they are unhappy, as attitudes about separation and divorce are more lenient. Blended families, alternative lifestyles, and single-parent homes are all common occurrences in America today.

These relationship options offer scenarios unseen in previous generations. I'm not a preacher, and I don't want to be one, but I have to talk to the men. Congratulations go out to all fathers who are doing what they know they should be doing for their families. Thank you for taking your rightful place in the family. Fatherhood is the most difficult job any man can have, but notice the word *difficult* does not mean *impossible*.

For some time now, critics have been downplaying African American fathers in this country more than they have been highlighting their good deeds. Black men, who are great fathers, are getting a bad name from those who have neglected their children. I know this firsthand because I was a single father who was criticized by women at my job. My female coworkers would make comments like, "A child should be with their mother," "A man can't do what a woman can." Out of all that criticism, no one ever said the child needed to be with both parents. I recall standing in the courtroom when the judge awarded me custody of my son. I was unable to locate his mother, so the divorce was treated as uncontested.

The judge looked down at me from behind a large oak bench and said, "The evidence shows that you are providing a safe and secure home environment and education for the child, and your finances seem to be in order. I am granting you custody of your son. Is there anything that you would like to say?"

"Yes, Your Honor, I would like to request child support from his mother," I stated.

The judge looked over the documents in front of her and then back at me with a smile on her face. She chuckled. "Mr. Young, it looks as though you have a very impressive yearly income as well as your military retirement, and with that, I believe you are more than capable of providing for yourself and your son. Therefore, I'm going to deny your request for child support," she announced.

I am certain that if my ex-wife had been there instead of me, the judge would have kicked me around that courtroom like a pair of dirty socks. I wanted to say something to her, but it would have landed me in jail for at least thirty days, so I kept my cool. I'm telling all of you men out there with custody of your children, and those of you who don't, to keep your cool.

If you are truly serious about being the leading man in your child's life, God will bless your request. If you have been denied child support or if you believe the payments you have been ordered to pay are too excessive, keep a level head. There are cases where child support payments that make it difficult for you to keep up with your bills have been lowered. If you can't afford a lawyer, you can seek pro bono (free) legal counsel.

I wrote a quote that reads, "Don't fight criticism because eventually criticism will destroy itself." What that means is don't get caught up arguing or becoming hateful toward the mother of your child. Instead, tap into the resources at the National Fatherhood Initiative website[xi] for more information on how to be involved in your child's life.

There is a myth that black men don't support their own and an old saying that says, "Actions speak louder than words." Don't worry about what is being said about black fathers. You are still the most valuable asset in your child's life and in the community. Instead, encourage your brothers who are not taking care of their children to handle their business. Come up with an action plan and do what's right to raise your children the right way.

## Support in Tough Times

The unemployment rate in the United States for white Americans is about 7 percent, as of October 2012. In the African American community, the rate has doubled that of whites in America at 14 percent.[xii] African Americans are not strangers to hard times; in fact, you can read any history book to understand the deep legacy of perseverance. The fact that poverty and unemployment are more pronounced in the black community does not mean men don't have anything to offer their families.

As a man, I am hardwired to be a provider, and just like other men, I understand the need to be able to afford things for my children. However, the truth is that I am no less of a man just because I was homeless and without a job. When I lost everything, I was consumed with the fact I had nowhere to go and no means of support for my son and myself. Yet it was my son who reminded me that despite our situation, there was no excuse for me not to maintain my responsibility as a father.

"Do what you need to do, Dad. I know you will fix this," he often said to me. Having custody of my son forced me to face reality, and with God's help, I lifted us out of poverty and into prosperity. You can do the same.

Single mothers have no choice but to look at their situation and try to find a way out because the father of their child is not around. Men, especially unemployed men, may find marriage and child-rearing a burden, but it costs very little to pick up a phone and call your child. "Research shows that the most important elements of raising children are time, attention, and resources" (Whitehead, 1993).[xiii]

If a man lacks in one area, he has the power within himself to increase his presence in the other two areas while looking to improve in the area of need. In the past, the extended family played a vital role in helping to raise children.

As previously stated, my grandmother was a significant member of my household and was a direct influence in our lives. I also grew up around uncles and cousins, all of whom provided rich social-learning experiences that enabled me to know how to treat others, how to have empathy, and how to be compassionate.

In America, there is a focus on the individual that helps to shape the idea of success at a young age. The "me" mentality is implanted in the psyche of our nation. Men who neglect their children reinforce this damaging mindset because in all truth, no one person can do anything alone, and a man who leaves his child opens the child up to the influence of forces that do not have the best interests of the child at heart. A child who grows up without a father and who, for any number of reasons, is separated from his extended family has not had the opportunity to form family connections nor cultivate proper relationship skills.

A man who, despite his poor finances, spends time with his children offers a connection that fosters lifelong affection. The power of choice is incredible! Disconnected families, fatherless homes, and single-parent households fall victim more often to alcohol, depression, drug use, high stress levels, and are many times breeding grounds for criminal intent and oppositional behaviors. Men, I promise you, there is no need to panic. You are more than capable of showing your children how to overcome a setback in life and teaching them a valuable lesson on how to be resilient and build strong character.

Whether you are living in the same house or not, your actions will provide a model of what a man should be in the eyes of your children. Let me give you an example. One day, my son and I were having dinner, and he asked me, "Dad, what is a father?" He caught me off guard. I wanted to know what he was thinking, so I asked him, "Do you think I'm a good father?" His reply was even more surprising. "That's not my question, Dad," he said.

I looked around, hoping to find the answer on the restaurant walls as the seconds ticked away. I took a breath and said, "A father is someone who is not just the biological creator in the father-child relationship—the father is the heart of the family. A father just doesn't run around making babies willy-nilly, but he stays long after the child is born. A father takes care of his children, contributing to their welfare. He participates in the child's life."

"You have been that and a lot more. I just need to know what to do if I should ever become a father," my son replied. Talk about a precious moment! Not only did my son require that I explain my belief system with regard to the definition of a father, but he acknowledged his appreciation of me in his life.

My son is now thirty-six years old, and he's accomplished many things as a productive member of society. My son and I did what almost all children and parents do when they spend time together: we bonded and solidified our relationship. As a single father, I made it a habit to look for opportunities that would help my son and I grow together.

I challenge all fathers to dig within yourselves and work harder at being better fathers. The streets are taking our children daily, and as fathers, we need to get more involved in the different activities, including homework, teaching our kids to cook, participating in sports and after-school programs, volunteer work in the community, and church. Attend the parent-teacher conferences, honor-roll assemblies, and school functions, and work with teachers and coaches to enhance the life of your child. I joined a group called Watch D.O.G.S. (Dads of Great Students). Check it out at www.fathers.com.[xiv]

## Step Up and Show Up

My older brother passed away in 1994. His son, my nephew, got married and had two sons. Shortly after they were born, my nephew asked me if I would step in as his sons' grandfather. My nephew made it very clear to his sons that I'm their great-uncle, but I am playing the role of both uncle and grandpa. They have accepted that fact, and depending on their mood, I'm either uncle-grandpa or grandpa-uncle.

They're in California and I make it a point to get out there as often as possible to visit. In addition to visiting, I call, send cards, and check in with my nephew and his family to make sure everything is okay. His sons have access to me, and I'm in their lives to offer advice and support, the way a grandfather or uncle should be.

Children need fathers in their lives, period! Bitter ex-wives can be a challenge; I know this for a fact, but it cannot serve as an excuse not to be involved. A man has to want to be a part of his children's lives, despite the odds against him. Men struggle after a breakup or divorce, and too often the separation from the mother of our children results in an inability to be an effective father. The time and energy required to sustain a nourishing relationship with our children is overwhelming when we are trying to establish a new household of our own. There are adjustments that must be made by everyone involved.

The cold reality of the entire issue of stepping up and being a father is that the alternative, single-mother households have become the norm. Poverty in single-parent homes can be detrimental to children, not because the parent loves their child any less or because they are not good parents, but because the cost of living is far too high to raise a child on one income and have enough time to dedicate to the child without being overwhelmed.

As incredible as women are, we have overworked and underpaid them in America and expect them to take on a full-time job, sometimes two jobs, and full-time parenting alone. It's not fair, and fathers need to do something about it. Children who spend time with both parents, even when the parents are no longer together, perform better in school and are less likely to fall prey to teen pregnancy, gangs, and other negative influences. Two parents provide access to love, guidance, advice, protection, and wisdom that facilitates better decision-making abilities in the child.

The Temptations song, "Papa was a Rollin' Stone," is a self-fulfilling prophecy. In fact, it has become commonplace for people to engage in casual sex and become pregnant without long-term committed relationships. According to Kids Count, an initiative of the Annie E. Casey Foundation in Baltimore, Maryland, "24 percent of white mothers, 66 percent of black mothers, 52 percent of American Indian mothers, and 41 percent of Latina mothers are raising children alone."[xv]

Earlier in the book, I stated that 72 percent of African American children in some states live in single-family homes. I need to clarify that this percentage is a breakdown by states that have a rate of single-parent homes at 70 percent or higher and includes: Arkansas, Illinois, Indiana, Kentucky, Michigan, Mississippi, Missouri, Louisiana, Ohio, Tennessee, Wisconsin, and Washington, DC. The average rate of single-parent homes nationwide in the black community is 66 percent. The Women's Legal Defense and Education Fund estimates in their 2012 report that 40 percent of single-mother families are poor and triple the poverty rate for the rest of the population.[xvi]

It should be stated that there are institutional differences in incarceration rates among blacks, Latinos, and whites that add to the issue of fatherless homes. To be fair to those men who, by their own choice, became involved with crime and cannot support their children, we will note the statistics presented by the NAACP: African Americans make up a little less than half of the 2.3 million prisoners nationwide.[xvii]

One in six black men has been incarcerated, while one-third of all black male children born today can anticipate being arrested and sentenced to prison sometime in their lives.[xvii] I do not mean to sound harsh, because I do understand the history of racial segregation and discrimination in the United States; however, the next statistic will explain why I'm angry with our criminal justice system. It's a fact that young African American kids who get in trouble in school are more likely to be referred to the police than other kids. According to an article in the *Huffington Post*, "The US Department of Justice (DOJ) reports 2.2 million people are in our nation's jails and prisons and another 4.5 million people are on probation or parole in the US, totaling 6.8 million people, one of every thirty-five adults."[xviii] Fourteen million whites and 2.6 million blacks report using street drugs. "Five times as many whites are using drugs as blacks, yet African Americans are sent to prison ten times more often."[xix]

Mandatory minimum sentencing disparities are responsible for the lockup of men in the black community. The article went on to read that for all drug arrests between 1980 and 2000, the black drug-arrest rate rose dramatically from 6.5 to 29. That's 1 per 1,000 persons. During the same period, the white drug-arrest rate barely increased from 3.5 to 4.6 per 1,000 persons.

My concern is that black men and today's youth are not reaching their potential because they are following the street life. Black men and white men, along with today's youth, are selling drugs rather than going to college and applying for jobs to impact the workforce. The Institute for Responsible Fatherhood and Family Revitalization reports that fatherless children are twenty times more likely to end up in prison compared to their peers raised in two-parent homes.[xx] The mission of the group is "turning the hearts of fathers unto their children."

In addition to my work, there are countless local, state, and national community groups and organizations dedicated to the issue of helping fathers take their rightful place in the home. There are no excuses! Proverbs 22:6 (ESV) puts it into perspective:

> *Train up a child in the way he should go, even when he is old and he will not depart from it.*

Or we can consult 1 Corinthians 13:11 (KJV):

> *When I was a child, I spoke as a child; I understood as a child, I thought as a child, but when I became a man, I put away childish things.*

## Real Dads Care

I had the opportunity to interview five young fathers who do not provide support for their children or the child's mother. Their excuses were the same as they said things like, "I can't find a job," and "Child support costs too much." These young men were stereotypical, with their sagging pants, flashy jewelry, freshly braided hair, and other material, designer urban wear.

While they maintain an image, their children are going without. Real Dads Network, an outgrowth of a documentary titled *Real Dads—Black Men on Fatherhood,* is one example of men focused on providing a support network for fathers. The vision statement of the organization is noble as they work to create a culture where all black fathers are actively involved in the parenting process and are portrayed and viewed as exemplary role models by society.[xxi]

Events, workshops, media, public policy, and advocacy are all areas addressed by this group. There is evidence that a movement in support of fatherhood is underway in America. Another example is The Real M.E.N.S. Project in Mississippi. If you recall, Mississippi was one of the states with

70 percent or higher single-parent homes. This group made their contribution by writing and publishing a limited-edition book made up of a collection of essays and photographs.[xxii] Bruce Gibbs, the publisher of *REAL DADS Magazine,* is a public speaker on the topics of fatherhood and preparing for college. His website offers links to articles, a newsletter, and T-shirts.[xxiii]

Let's take a look at the national initiatives on improving the presence of fathers in the lives of their children. The National Fatherhood Initiative is a leading source for research on the cost of absent fathers to society. Their work is community based and includes media appearances to engage organizations and raise awareness of the issue. They've partnered with corporations to create a special relationship with the United States military in order to offer the Military Fatherhood Awards.[xxiv]

The best thing about the Internet is the unlimited access to information and instant connections to others who are working to promote responsible fatherhood. The only thing required is courage to take the first step and try.

## Your Child's First Influences

Research has shown that between birth and three years of age, a child undergoes a series of fundamental emotional developments.[xxv] According to the Michigan Department of Community Health (MDCH), early years "set the stage for all future development."[xxi] The quality of these early relationships has a far more significant influence on early learning than has previously been understood. (You need to understand that your child is profoundly influenced by you.) The types of movies the child watches, the music the child listens to, and the amount of books read and homework done all influence that child. The diet and amount of play and exercise, and the types of communication, whether positive or negative—every detail, the child absorbs and models.[xxvi]

The Administration for Children and Families, a division of the United States Department of Health and Human Services, is home to the Child Welfare Information Gateway project. (The website offers publications and a wealth of information from legislation to available services. There are videos, web links, and print resources on all topics related to child welfare and well-being).[xxvii]

Start today to be your child's most relevant instructor of life by getting to know your child. Spending time with a child at the park or drawing a picture opens up opportunities for conversation and the transfer of knowledge. If you are an adult who is busy in the world and not available for your children, then you have to do a self-assessment today and find ways to connect with your child. Cooking and eating meals together, bedtime rituals such as quiet reading or talking about the events of the day, or playtime can be small chunks of time during the day that allow for genuine bonding to take place. But let me leave you with this:

*Don't stick it out there if you are afraid of responsibility.*

—Dr. Carlton N. Young

## It Still Takes a Village to Raise a Child

There is an African proverb that states, "It takes a village to raise a child." This can also be used for all races, not just the African American community. If you watch the news on any day, you will see that all children of all ethnic groups need the support of their entire community, or "village."

When we read about children who are killing other children, or when we hear about twelve-year-olds having babies, or the rise of high school dropouts, or the increase of our youth being in prison, this is a clear message that the community needs to step up and do its part to save our children. I am involved with many organizations that provide youth support. I am doing my part as an elder in the "village."

My mission as America's Grandfather is to provide youth and adults with a person whom they can come to for advice, to talk to, and just share their dreams and hopes with. I want to become the role model for other men who will also take their place as leaders in their homes and in their communities. When I think of this subject, two people come to mind. The first is the late Dr. Myles Munroe, who was an international teacher, speaker, lecturer, and evangelist. Dr. Munroe was the founder and president of Bahamas Faith Ministries International. He was a best-selling author, and in his book *In Pursuit of Purpose*, he makes a quote: "Until purpose is discovered, existence has no meaning, for purpose is the source of fulfillment."[xxviii] So when I look at our young men and women today and the direction a lot of them are headed, it tells me that they have not discovered their purpose in life. Why is that?

As parents, we have not come together as one force in our homes, in the lives of our children, in our children's schools, and in our communities. We have to help our youth understand what purpose really means. Purpose is vision, and vision encourages goals that develop the purpose for the pursuit of life.

Growing up, my brother and I, along with my cousin, would get together with the other kids in the neighborhood during the summer months, and we would all go to the school and play football, basketball, and baseball. These were known as the neighborhood grudge matches.

One thing that would always happen was any parent from any home would come out and tell us, "Okay, it's time for you boys to go home now," and without any hesitation, we would all pick up and head for home. There would also be times when our little brother or sister would yell out and say, "Daddy said it's time for everybody to go home!"

Back then when I was growing up, communities had a purpose for their existence and fulfillment for the lives of their youth. Every household on every street looked out for each child of every neighborhood.

The second person that comes to mind is the best-selling author of *Success Runs in Our Race*, George C. Fraser, the man who came up with the phrase, "Each one, reach one, teach one." "It takes a village to raise a child" does not imply that you the parent are incapable of raising your child. What it implies is that we are and should be responsible for how our local, state, and federal governments develop the educational process that maintains our schools, cities, and the strength to educate our children.

I believe that when we all are involved in the education of every child in our community, our children have a much better chance for success in their lives. Parents, without a doubt, make the best teachers outside of the educational institution for raising their children because of their authority as the parent. Remember: Each one, reach one, teach one.

## My Advice to Educators Who Teach Children

*The Commonwealth requires the education of the people as the safeguard of order and liberty.*

—Boston Public Library, Boylston Street

Teachers are the most underpaid and under respected people on this planet. Many do what they do because of the passion they have for education, and not for the money. Our teachers in America work in the classrooms across this country and deserve to be paid as much as a doctor would be paid. These teachers provide healing to the mind just like doctors provide healing for the body.

In my day, a teacher was a respected person and had the power and the authority to be an extension of the family. The educator is a person who serves as a leading member of the community, whether you think so or not. As educators, you undertake the serious responsibility and the legal obligation to communicate to the children and their families the need for a better education.

As educators, you must love what you do, love what you teach, and be passionate about what you're teaching and how you teach it. Know the children and their individual and social developmental needs, from their physical and emotional needs to their spiritual ones.

I myself was not an exceptional student in high school. Actually, the night of my high school graduation, after I received my diploma, my mother told me, "You only graduated because they need your desk and the space for next year!" I thought that was a bold statement and very disturbing that my mother would say or think that of me.

Just like in any other profession, great educators are overshadowed by the bad. The testing scandal in Atlanta, Georgia, gave our Atlanta-area schools and educators a bad name even though every school and educator was not involved in the scandal. I've seen this time after time where great educators are punished for the bad deeds of school administrators.

As an educator, you must first realize that you are the only positive source to a child that is having learning difficulties, so you can't allow outside negativity to destroy your creativity in the classroom. There's a quote by Aristotle: "The roots of education are bitter, but the fruit is sweet."

Known for yourself why you have chosen to become an educator, and then love being an educator. Now that you have this information at hand, I would suggest that you share it with your students. As educators, you may need to communicate more than just the importance of getting an education to our children.

What I mean by that is our children need to understand that you, the educator, care—care about the balance of emotion in their lives. Demonstrate more understanding when it comes to applying behavioral conduct and expectations in the classrooms and hallways of our learning institutions. Use good communication techniques that are consistent, and please don't assume you know the child's thoughts, feelings, and the reasons for their behavior. Develop a working relationship with your students, and remember that a good working relationship does not require the approval of shared values.

*Teaching is not a lost art, but the regard for it is a lost tradition.*

—Jacques Barzun

The above quote is one of the most truthful sayings about our educational system. There has been an increase over the years, in our children and in some parents, of the disregard for educators and the educational system.

I was visiting one of the high schools in the Atlanta area doing my research for this book and observed one of the most disturbing and disrespectful acts by a student toward a teacher I have seen in years. The disrespect came when the student was walking down the hallway to their classroom.

The student had a pair of headphones on, listening to music (which is against the school's rules). The teacher made an attempt to stop the student and tell them to take off the headset and place it in their locker. The student ignored the request and basically walked over her by using his height, body weight, and muscular size to force the teacher out of his way.

What was really disturbing was that he seemed to not have cared that there were visitors on the school grounds or the consequences for his actions. When I saw this act of disrespect, it pushed me to do more research. I found that some bad behavior in our schools is sometimes created by parents who are overindulgent and have behavioral problems themselves. Behavioral problems have gotten worse over the past years. But the best advice I can give you, the educator, comes from my mother-in-law, who was a schoolteacher in the state of New York.

After working for a very large law firm for more than twenty-six years, she became an educator at age forty-six, and for the next twenty-five years lived her passion. I put her advice in the following quote:

> *The best advice I can give to teachers is to first realize that teaching is one of the most rewarding professions.*
>
> *—Doris E. Parker*
> *Retired Educator*

You must first have a love for children and enjoy being with them. Understand how each child learns, and to do this, you need to always be in control of your classroom. Know how to inspire a child to do their best at all times. An "indefinable person," that's you! Become the person that children naturally respect and admire. Always set an example on how to behave; start with yourself.

One thing you should always remember is that being patient and keeping a positive attitude will help when dealing with difficult parents. When looking at your own personal development toward what you do, always keep an open mind toward new things to learn. Never say, "It's too late."

Your personal development should never become an attempt for perfection. Realize this: You are not perfect—no one is—because we all make mistakes.

> *Anyone who has never made a mistake has never tried anything new.*
>
> –Albert Einstein

So work at being enthusiastic, organized, knowledgeable, and efficient in your field of education and enjoy the subject you teach.

## Seek Support

Seek support from your colleagues, because I think maybe there comes a time when we all get complacent and we forget what excited us about our jobs in the first place. It might be time to start asking for new advice from your colleagues. They may be able to recommend new tips you can use in your classroom.

As a motivational speaker, I have found that motivation is the inner power of your energy that propels you into action toward achievement. When I got started in the public-speaking business, I had some of the most experienced mentors: Less Brown, Kevin Bracy, Donna "Serious" Satchell, and Norma Thompson Hollis, just to name a few. They were excellent! It's always a good thing to surround yourself with knowledgeable professionals in your field of education.

Keep your students informed that you are in this endeavor for a better education together. I'm sure they will enjoy assisting you. Always show enthusiasm and share with your students what you have learned and experienced. Observe what good teachers do, and ask questions. Use the Internet as a resource tool, use the school library, and encourage your students to do the same. Learn how the school system works and also how students learn and interact by volunteering.

These are great tips that a teacher will find useful in the classroom. Remember to track your performance, and I suggest positive change along the way.

## My Message to the Criminal Justice System

> *Justice is certain rectitude of mind whereby a man does what he ought to do in the circumstances confronting him.*
>
> —Thomas Aquinas

Let me ask this question: is the law a source of ethical standards? When it comes down to family, children, parents, custody, guardianship, and child support, I believe the criminal justice system is one sided. Here is my assessment of what I think, and I'm speaking from my own experience: we have allowed the justice system to be controlled by our youth and not by the powers that be.

When a child knows that he or she will not face any con- sequences in the home, the parent moves to the back of the line. The justice system has replaced the head of household, the working father, and the single working mother (the taxpayers and the supporters of the child) with a child.

You have come into the homes of millions of families across the country and taken the power and authority of parenting away from the home. Either you can't see it or you have realized that you have made the biggest mistake since the Jheri curl. I believe that the decision you have made under your "criminal justice system" title has had a devastating effect on the state of American families. Your system has allowed our children to take matters into their own hands and not question the consequences.

In 1992, I was told by our justice system—and the Department of Human Resources Division of Family and Children Services—that I had no power to stop my daughter from dropping out of school, and when I say justice system, I'm talking about the ones who write the new laws that "protect" our youth from Mama and Daddy. Yes, there are some parents and adults running around that our children need protecting from; that's a given. But when you come into my house and tell me—the parent, the taxpayer, the breadwinner, and let's not forget, the registered voter—that my child was old enough to make their own decision about their education without my permission, you've crossed the line.

My daughter was fifteen years old when she dropped out of school, and there was nothing I could do about it. Now here's the twist: My daughter was allowed to drop out of school, and I was told I would still be responsible for her actions because she was a minor. My child was old enough at fifteen to make the decision that she no longer wanted to go to school and get an education, but when it came to running the streets without supervision, I was responsible for her actions because the law said she was still a minor.

Nationwide, the common age for a child to legally drop out of school is sixteen. There are about nine states that require compulsory schooling until seventeen. I was in a conversation about this subject maybe a year ago with a young man who dropped out of school, and his defense was that he needed instant money. My answer to his defense was that making money is one thing; knowing how to count it is another!

The system has in place child labor laws that once a child reaches the age of eighteen, he or she is no longer subject to the federal youth employment and child labor laws. But now during the school year, hours are limited to three hours a day and eighteen hours a week for children ages fourteen to seventeen.

In the summer and on days when there's no school, working hours increase to eight hours a day and forty hours a week. But the labor law also limits when a child can work, and that's until 7:00 p.m. But if the same child wants to fight their parents, walk out of the home, hang out, and come back when they please, there is not much the parent can do.

If I put that belt to that behind, then the criminal justice system says I am an abusive parent. The really bad part about it is you have some parents who agree with the system because they gave up and quit. However, my research about the criminal justice system indicates that after an alarming rise in crime over a number of years since 2006, "the number of young adults ages eighteen to twenty-nine in prison or jail fell by 11 percent between 2008 and 2009."[xxix] Spending time in prison or jail can have profound effects on a young person's future. Up to one-third of incarcerated youth return to jail or prison within a few years after release. [xxix]

Two important issues are associated with youth imprisonment and the disproportionate representation of minorities.

According to the Bureau of Justice Statistics, "one in three black men can expect to go to prison in their lifetime."[xxx] According to the American Civil Liberties Union (ACLU), "Individuals of color have a disproportionate number of encounters with law enforcement, indicating that racial profiling continues to be a problem." [xxxi]

The second issue is that students of color face harsher punishments in school than their white peers. In a report by the Center for American Progress, black and Hispanic students represent more than 70 percent of those involved in school-related arrests or referrals to law enforcement.[xxxii] The Southern Coalition for Social Justice reported in April 2014 that one in three African American men can expect to be incarcerated at some point. These statistics reflect systemic problems in the US justice system, leading to a higher number of youth of color being incarcerated.[xxxiii] Currently, African Americans make up two-fifths, and Hispanics one-fifth of confined youth today. Youth who have been incarcerated experience diminished incomes in comparison with their non-incarcerated peers.[xxxiv] The findings are as predictable as they are disturbing.

In an article by Prison Policy Initiative, "the American prison system is bursting at the seams with people who have been shut out of the economy and who had neither a quality education nor access to good jobs. We found that in 2014, incarcerated people had a median annual income of $19,185 prior to their incarceration, which is 41 percent less than non-incarcerated people of similar ages. Economic hardship in turn is associated with lower levels of mental well-being, physical health, social attachments, and a lower life expectancy."[xxxv]

Now I understand that each individual has to be responsible for their own actions, and I'm not saying that the criminal justice system makes an individual do wrong. What I am saying is that the laws and the lawmakers that allow our children to make decisions as adults when they are clearly not capable of doing so need to start looking at the results of that law.

There are stark racial disparities in the population of incarcerated youth. Among the estimated 778,200 young adults ages eighteen to twenty-nine who were incarcerated in mid-2009, 40 percent (314,100) were black.[xxxvi] Research was conducted by Ashley Nellis, a senior research analyst with the Sentencing Project, a Washington, DC–based nonprofit that promotes reforms in criminal justice policy. The report, published in June 2016, reads that black Americans were incarcerated in state prisons at an average rate of 5.1 times that of white Americans.

For example, in 2009, among men ages twenty to twenty-four, 9.8 percent of blacks were incarcerated, followed by 3.7 percent of Hispanics and 1.6 percent of whites. Among women, a higher percentage of blacks were incarcerated than women of other races, although racial/ethnic differences among women are smaller than among men.[xxxvii]

The number of adult women incarcerated has increased over the last three decades, and women of color have been disproportionately represented. The racial and ethnic disparities are startling. African

American women are three times more likely than white women to be incarcerated, while Hispanic women are 69 percent more likely than white women to be incarcerated.[xxxviii]

## General Dropout Statistics

Since each state has its own laws that allow children to drop out of school without their parents' permission, according to a *Huffington Post* report in January 2012, "I'm dropping out" are the words spoken by roughly a quarter of American high school students. A student becomes a dropout every nine seconds in America. That's approximately one in four students.[xxxix]

Once a student reaches the age set by the law, he/she is no longer required by law to go to school. As a general rule, a student that meets the dropout age requirement for that state doesn't need permission from his/her parents nor the school to drop out. Nationwide, nearly one in three US high school students fails to graduate with a diploma. In total, approximately 1.2 million students fail to graduate high school each year, averaging 7,000 students every school day, or 1 every 26 seconds, over half of whom are minorities. Dropouts cost the United States $260 billion in lost wages, taxes, and productivity over their lifetime. If graduation rates of minorities rise to the levels of whites by year 2020, personal incomes would add more than $330 billion to the United States economy.[xl]

Give the power of parenthood back to the family.

## Family Value #6

# Family Uncertainty – Dealing with Doubt and Times of Uncertainty

Most of us look to our families for security, comfort, support, and love. Throughout all of that, every family has its faults. We can say that families should stick together through thick and thin, no matter what! But let's be real; that's not the case all of the time.

When the American family runs into trouble—whether it's money troubles, marriage problems, you name it—most of us don't like to expose our family problems to other family members or friends if something is wrong. We cover it up! When your family problems are not that big, this might not cause much harm, but sometimes they can grow and get out of hand, creating more problems later down the road.

Dealing with uncertainty comes in all forms. I was single for most of my adult life and loved it. But when I met and married my wife, I experienced the loss of being a single person, the freedom to go and come as I wished and sleep in for as long as I liked. Sleeping helped me through the uncertainty of being married. But as we grew, so did our relationship and our commitment to each other. (I had to put that in here; she's going to read the book too.)

Uncertainty comes like a thief in the night, changing everyone in the family. When I shifted from being single to being married, I experienced some loss, but through all the uncertainty of being married, I came to understand that it was a process that comes after the honeymoon. Not just a destination, uncertainty can be and is one of life's sobering moments. When it comes to doubt and times of uncertainty, like most people, we went into married life on a wave of affection that occasionally gave us some self-doubt and apprehension, but with trust, love, and understanding, it only rises again to become stronger than ever.

## Dealing with the Unknown

When I was diagnosed with cancer, uncertainty consumed me, and fear was my closest friend. The doctors told my wife that cancer changes everyone in the family. Well, I beg to differ. Cancer changes the outlook of one's health. The uncertainty of having cancer for me was not knowing if my treatments were working or not. The hardest part of living with cancer for me was the treatments. I told myself every day that I had cancer, not the other way around.

One thing you should know if you don't already is that uncertainty and doubt are familiar in our families and in our homes. When the doctor told me one thing about my cancer, I always heard something else, so my wife had to tell me what the doctor was really saying. I said that to say this: As a people, we all hear one thing, but we see another. This makes it true that doubt and uncertainty are common in our lives. By keeping a positive attitude, I removed the toxic negativity from my thinking, and now I'm living cancer-free.

## Motivating the Motivator

I recently wrote an article for the Toastmasters club of West Georgia on the power of speech and leadership. I wrote about being in combat and the uncertainty men and women in our military face day after day. But it's communication that motivates us into action. The month of October 2012, Superstorm Sandy left power outages and millions homeless in her wake. After the dangerous winds and rains passed, it left uncertainty in the lives of the families affected by the storm, which were now in the hands of our government.

People crave leadership most during periods of chance and uncertainty. The people in need can be the source of motivation for local leaders until they all get back to normal. But let's not look at uncertainty only in the negative. There's a quote by Jacob Bronowski that reads, "Knowledge is an unending adventure at the edge of uncertainty." What this means is that you should have the confidence to motivate yourself when you think you can't motivate your family.

# Family Health Care

## Creating a Family Health History

Do you know how important your family health history is? It's not only important to you, but for your children as well. For years, I never knew what my family health history was. In fact, it wasn't until after my older brother passed away that I realized not just me, but my nephew and my son had no idea what our family health history was.

Look, you walk into the doctor's office and he starts to ask questions about your family, but you can't give him an answer because you don't know. The surgeon general and the US Department of Health and Human Services have a campaign called the Surgeon General's Family History Initiative to inspire all American families to learn about their family health history.

I encourage all of you to take part in this campaign, even if it's not for your own personal interest. Make it for your family's health. Why do you need to collect your family health history? We all should collect our family's health information for our health care providers because they have no other way of diagnosing what is going on with our health.

We all have been asked by our doctors to describe our family medical history during an appointment. But if you have not gotten any information about your family members' past health problems (your mother/father/grandparents), you can be missing the vital information that your doctor may need to provide you with the proper care. Now, if you don't have this information, you need to start working on getting it. Families all talk about their family tree; well, now let's start talking about what I call the "family health tree."

I started one for my family and my nephew and his two sons. It was something our family had needed for years. It's not hard to get started. Start where you are with the information you have; list names, dates of birth, health issues, doctor's names, and hospital care. If you know the history and the reason of death of a family member, you will need to record that as well, along with your emergency contact numbers.

## The Uncertainty of Smoking, Alcohol, HIV/AIDS, and STDs

We all know that regular health exams help find and/or prevent most problems before they start. That's nothing more than preventive maintenance, just like taking care of your car before a long road trip. That brings me to this point: we will give our cars, boats, clothing, and in some cases our pets a checkup before we do what we need to do for ourselves.

We all have known for years that smoking is bad for our health, and now we know that secondhand smoke from the cigarettes of smokers is also dangerous and can kill. And yet we still smoke. Also, there is growing evidence by the National Council on Alcoholism and Drug Dependence that alcoholism has a genetic component. Alcohol abuse is a problem that either directly or indirectly causes two million deaths each year. In a 1989 article by the National Institute on Alcohol Abuse and Alcoholism, alcoholism often seems to run in families, and we may hear about some studies of an "alcoholism gene." Genetics certainly influence our likelihood of developing alcoholism, but the story isn't that simple.

Research shows that genes are responsible for about half of the risk for alcoholism. Therefore, genes alone do not determine whether someone will become an alcoholic. Environmental factors, as well as gene and environment interactions, account for the remainder of the risk. When we take on the conversations about the risk of infections, HIV, STDs, and AIDs, do we really know the basic facts? When talking to our children about having premarital sex, I believe that a parent should ask this question to themselves before asking their child if they understand about sexually transmitted diseases. We as parents should seek out more information and ask questions on the most common STDs among our youth today.

## I Don't Have a Problem

People who drink and are unable to control their drinking may have a drinking problem, but are not willing to admit that they may have an addiction. Unfortunately, there are people whose social drinking has led to heavier drinking and other problems. Think about this question: have you ever done anything you may regret doing because you were intoxicated (drunk)? Whatever it was, think on this: "It was never supposed to happen." That's called binge drinking, and it's a big problem. During my military career, I knew guys who loved to drink but were unable to stop once they got started.

At one point in my military career, I served in the family services advocate's office as the drug, alcohol, and suicide counselor for both marine and navy personnel and their families. I was able to see firsthand the people who love drinking but were not alcoholics. There were men and women who had to go to recovery but didn't drink that much; they just could not handle the effects of alcohol. Read this! If you drink alcohol, try to limit your intake, and always eat something when you drink. But do this for me: Please check with your doctor and ask if alcohol is safe for you to drink. We are talking about having a drink. I like to have a drink every now and then. The real problem is not the drinking; it's not knowing when to stop drinking. Since the introduction of alcohol and drinking into our communities, every culture has been affected. It alters our mental state, so when some jerk is able to introduce a new beverage, a new form of plant, or a vapor, it's only because they realized that the uncontrolled use of that drug has one purpose, and that's to give you a buzz, take control over your life, and leave you with nothing but potential problems.

## Diabetes, You, and Alcohol

I'm talking about our health, yours and mine. I have seen the inside of a hospital emergency room about five times this year alone, so I have a lot of concerns about the health of the American family and their social life. Yes, I take a little "nip" now and again, but not to the point where it could affect my health and my medical condition.

I would like to say to those who may have diabetes, my friend had an uncle who passed away about five or six years ago from diabetes. He was a great guy, but he would never follow through on his doctor's advice. He was not an alcoholic, just a man who I thought might have done more social drinking than he should have. I don't know, but that could have caused him some health problems.

If you are a diabetic and are taking medications that lower your blood glucose, you need to be very cautious not only about your drinking, but also about your food intake. Before you eat or drink, make sure you check your blood glucose before you go to bed.

I was on a flight from Anchorage, Alaska, back to Atlanta in September of 2012 when I felt a little light-headed. We were about two and a half hours into a five-hour flight when I decided to get up and go to the bathroom. I remember getting up out of my seat and stepping into the aisle; the next thing I remembered was waking up in the emergency room in a hospital in Phoenix, Arizona.

What took place is that I did not take my medications before leaving Atlanta for Anchorage, Alaska, because I thought I could be back—on what was to be a turnaround trip—in time to take my medications. Turns out it was not a good idea. At that time, I was taking blood thinners and giving myself injections of enoxaparin and other medications. To top it off, I had nothing to eat for almost nine-plus hours. I kept telling myself that I would grab something to eat, but I never found the time.

The end result was my blood glucose dropped to its lowest level, therefore causing me to pass out. All this took place without alcohol being a factor. In short, what I'm saying is make sure you take your medications on time, eat, and stay hydrated!

## Sexual Health

When we talk about sexually transmitted diseases (STDs) today, they have become so common in our society that it's a wonder we're not having sex with each other like in the movie *Demolition Man* with Sylvester Stallone. The movie predicted high-level violence, self-driving cars, teleconferences, and tablet computers, all of which everyone is using in their day-to-day lives. But above all, it introduced "sexting," where Sylvester Stallone and the young lady wore computer-generated helmets over their heads to have sex by what they imagined they were doing without any physical contact.

We need to reach out to our children and explain to them on a higher level about sexually transmitted diseases before we hear them talking about sex. Now, I am totally against our youth having underage sex and the system giving out condoms. But not talking to them about it is giving them a hall pass to explore their sexuality and their sexual orientations without caution. One thing I know for sure is that when we talk to our youth about STDs, we are talking mostly HIV and AIDS, and that is a good thing. However, I caution you not to leave out other diseases like gonorrhea and chlamydia and so on.

Talk with your kids and make sure they have not put themselves at risk by doing something they know nothing about. There are so many different infections and sexually transmitted diseases that our youth are not aware of. As we all know, in the medical community they are making life-changing progress as they learn more about how HIV effects the immune system. What our youth, our children, may not understand is that STDs and other virus are spread through having unprotected vaginal and/or anal sex. Now I know earlier I said I was against giving out condoms to our youth—to me, this just helps encourage them to have sex, especially when our youth are as promiscuous as they are today. But condoms, if used correctly, can protect from all kinds of STDs, as well as unwanted pregnancies.

## Diabetes, Prostate Cancer, and Your Blood: Early Detection Saves Lives

How common is prostate cancer? And what causes it? I served on the board of the Georgia Prostate Cancer Coalition (GPCC), a nonprofit organization teaching men and their families about risk factors of prostate cancer and the importance of early detection. In a 2014 report by the American Cancer Society, one in four black men are more likely to get prostate cancer in their lives than other men, who have a one in eight chance of getting prostate cancer. But what is prostate cancer, and what causes it? It is when cancer cells grow on the prostate gland and quickly and aggressively spread to other areas of the body. Researchers don't really know exactly what causes this cancer, but they have found some risk factors and are trying to understand just how these factors cause prostate cells to become cancerous. For prevention and early detection, visit your doctor.

Now, the reasons for these differences are still unclear. Going back to the family history, that suggests that if your father or brother was diagnosed with prostate cancer, this more than doubles your risk of developing this disease.

The risk is much higher for families that may have had several male relatives who were diagnosed with prostate cancer, particularly if their relatives were young at the time they were diagnosed. Once again, we go back to our family history. It has been documented over the years that most men who are diagnosed with prostate cancer don't have a family history.

For those of you men who never had a checkup and don't think you will ever be diagnosed with this cancer, let me give you this small piece of information. Prostate cancer is the leading cause of cancer-related deaths in men in the United States. Early-detection screening is used to help find cancers or other diseases that may not yet have any outward symptoms.

Screening for prostate cancer is done by what is called a prostate-specific antigen (PSA) blood test and digital rectal exam (DRE). According to the American Cancer Society, the discussion to start testing should begin around age fifty for men who are at average risk of getting prostate cancer and have at least a ten-year life expectancy.[xli] My personal opinion on the subject of prevention and early detection is testing should start at age forty-five. This especially applies to men at high risk of developing prostate cancer. Start testing at age forty-five, but you should also know that prostate cancer is not always life threatening.

There have been studies on men who have died from other causes and whose autopsies reported that they had prostate cancer, but it never caused them problems during their life. In a study by the American Cancer Society and the Prostate Conditions Education Council (PCEC), one in every seven men will be diagnosed with prostate cancer during their lifetime, but only one man in thirty-four will die from the disease.[xlii]

So men, but more so to the wives of the men who might be reading this book, I need you to start talking to your doctors about getting checkups and start looking into your family history. I need you to start talking to other men in your family and in your community about how important it is to talk to your doctors about prostate cancer and a screening test.

## It's in the Blood

Whenever you go to the doctor's office, one of the first things they do is take your blood sample. We are diagnosed through our blood for whatever we think is wrong. I believe that a person can live longer, look better, and feel great if he or she has the proper nutrition and supplementation in their diet. Your blood doesn't lie! There have been numerous studies that show that a diet high in fruits and vegetables (and plenty of antioxidants) is associated with a lower incidence of macular degeneration. Blood tests (blood work) can show you what's in your blood. That's because the blood gives us insight into what we can't see from the outside.

Our blood is the transport system of nutrition to our body. With that, doctors use our blood work to assess our overall health.

## When the Family Loses a Loved One

We all have lost a loved one at some time in our lives. I should know, because I lost my father in 1983, my older brother in 1994, and my mother in 2006. The one thing I always heard people say to the family was, "If you need anything, call me." I would think to myself, *I'm the one who lost someone dear to me; you should be calling me to see if I need anything.* I realized what was being put off by the people who would say that. They are not being insensitive; they just don't know how to handle that much grief.

See, it's really difficult to help someone through their grieving after the loss of a loved one. What you need to do in this case is make sure that whoever is suffering from the loss has everything they need. This is a tough time, and that family member is going to need all the love and support you can give. Stop by and take them for a walk, and you know as well as I do a good walk can change the mood of anyone's attitude. Give the family your physical affection like hugs, taking their hand and just holding it, and even helping out around their house.

I don't need to tell a woman this, but maybe just in case there are some men who still have not caught on yet: some women will miss that physical touch, that closeness of that loved one, especially if that loved one was a son or husband. The most important thing you can do as a family member or friend is to listen when they want to talk.

## Family Value #7

# Healthy Lifestyle

Former First Lady Michelle Obama's health plan for our schools and children is the best I have ever heard. Her plan of action is to develop a strategy to ensure that our children have nutritional food and lunches to eat instead of fatty foods. We also have our own responsibility to educate not only our children, but ourselves to eat healthy and right.

I can't believe it took this long for someone to come down from the White House to tell us what we already knew. I agree with the former first lady that we need to eat more vegetables, fruits, and protein while cutting back on our sodium intake. Choose whole-grain foods, and when you shop, shop smartly and build a healthy meal for your family daily.

## Guide for a Healthy Lifestyle

More families need to stop talking about changing their lifestyle and actually change it to a healthier one. But as we all know, few people or families commit to making that change. One thing about this section is that although I am talking family, change is an individual action as well. You have to set your own goals to make the changes you need to make in your life and in the life of your family. Here are some healthy changes we need to make for our families' lifestyles:

**Exercise:** I think exercising has been the number-one way an individual or our families have started to make that change for a healthier lifestyle.

**Eating healthier:** What we eat has an effect on the quality of our lives and on the quality of our families. By not eating healthy, you deprive your body of its much-needed energy, and when you don't have the energy, you deprive your family of you.

**Stress:** Don't say life can be stressful, because I'm sure we all know about that. But how do we get through the stressful times? You need to know how to manage it. If you can't manage your stress, it will cause you to create more stress on your family than needed. Stress happens to everyone. We can't avoid our day-to-day lives, the bills, the kids, our jobs. The best we can do is learn to manage that day-to-day stress. It's of my own opinion that eating healthy, exercising regularly, and getting enough rest—just taking care of yourself on a regular basis—can help keep the signs of stress from your face and body. Stress can have an effect on your appearance.

## Family Value #8

# Family Basic Training 101

For years, I would ask myself, "Why am I here, and what is my purpose in this life?" Have you ever asked yourself this question? Well, I'm asking it again, but about the American family. As families move through the cycle of life, they are going through what I call their basic training for marriage, children, divorce, and emotional issues.

## Saving the Families

When I talk about saving the families, I look at it from a biblical aspect. The purpose here is to promote the betterment of the American family. We need to go into our communities and promote workshops, outreach programs, and family health and wellness programs. One other way I found to help save the family is to create a community organization that helps your community seek out new ways to bring better education and books into your schools.

Earlier in the book, I told you about the television show called *Save My Son*. This is something communities all over this country should have been doing years ago, in my opinion. We don't get involved today like our parents did years ago. I think it's time to get involved the old-fashioned way: one parent, one family, one child, and one community at a time.

Your family should be the symbol of all American families, and that symbol represents hope and prosperity. Within the black family structure, there was a study (Roberts, 2004) that stated over half of incarcerated black men with children lived with those children before incarceration. So, any emotional and economic support provided by that father had been removed, and the family's structure was destabilized by the removal of these fathers.

The growth of female-headed families is connected to the deep sex-ratio imbalances and the loss of marriageable men in many black communities (Wilson, 1987). This is an important factor in the growth of female single-parent family structures. We will explore this subject in Volume Two of the America's Grandfather series.

## Family Bank Accounts: The Financial Statistics of the American Family

A large percentage of America's families is relying on high-interest bank loans to buy homes, cars, or just to be able to catch up. But there is a very large percentage of family homes that don't have bank accounts, or they use check-cashing services and other alternatives to keep money in the home. I know I was one of those people who had lost everything and had to do whatever I could to bring a paycheck home. If you don't have a bank account, you need to get one started ASAP.

There were surveys done by several banking institutions: Black Enterprise Wealth for Life, the FDIC National Survey, and the Federal Reserve Bank. They reported that 21.4 percent of black families and 20.1 percent of Hispanic families didn't have bank accounts.[xliii] The average American family's savings account balance is about $3,800.[xliv] The percentage of American families with less than $1,000 in savings accounts is up to 69 percent.[xlv]

## Family Time: YMCA, Boy Scouts, Girl Scouts, and Family Outings

My wife and I love to travel and vacation. We love to get up and get out, but there are not a lot of families doing that these days. We have truly lost the family time. To improve yourself and your family's foundation, you have to get away from time to time. And if you can't leave town, you always have the YMCA for good family fun. As a family you can start using your local YMCA, or enroll your sons and daughters into the Boy Scouts and Girl Scouts. These are the places I recommend when trying to bring value back into your child's life and back into your home.

For years, the YMCA has accomplished its mission of putting Christian principles into practice through programs that build a healthy spirit, mind, and body for all young people. With a commitment to nurturing the potential of all children, promoting healthy living, and fostering a sense of social responsibility, the YMCA ensures that every individual has access to the essential skills needed to learn, grow, and succeed.

There is a statement about family time on the official site at YMCA.net by the YMCA that reads:

> The Y has always been a place where families can play and be active together. That's why we provide opportunities to bring families together to strengthen bonds and build lasting relationships. At the Y, families can share recreational activities, learn new skills, and just have fun being together. Don't wait, your children will be grown before you know it.

The Boy Scouts have a lot to offer a young man. The Boy Scouts gives the exposure to a uniquely hands-on learning experience through earning merit badges that reflect each boy's budding interests and unlock a world of discovery around them, prove his leadership skills, gain the confidence he needs to excel in life, in the world, and forge a path for his future.

For our young daughters, there's the Girl Scouts as well. With the Girl Scouts, they will do more than you ever thought they would; they will dream bigger dreams than they ever imagined. It's the Girl Scouts leadership experience, a collection of activities and experiences. As they go on exciting trips and explore the great outdoors, they will discover who they are, find their real interests and talents, and will get involved with great action projects that will make a difference in their lives for their future.

## Your Children Pulling Their Weight

My oldest granddaughter was visiting with my wife and me for just a very short time. But in that short period of time, she had trouble pulling her weight. So I ask you, is your child pulling their weight? This is where the child's discipline and independence should begin to start.

It was hard for us to get our granddaughter to pull her own weight. This comes from families not requiring their children to do household chores—no wonder our children have such a behavior problem. It was like pulling teeth to get my granddaughter to clean her room and put her things away when she would come to visit. When a child pulls his or her weight by doing what they are told, this development helps with the child's self-discipline and self-confidence.

## Mothers, Teach Your Sons to Grocery Shop

Moms, the time is here. You have to start teaching your sons how to take care of themselves. They should learn how to wash and iron clothes and how to wash the dishes after a meal. I went to visit some friends who live out of town, and my friend asked me to go with him to drop something off for his son. Not a problem, so I thought. We climbed into his car, went over to his son's apartment, and when we got there, my friend asked me if I would help bring some bags into his son's apartment. The long and short of it is we took about nine bags of groceries into the apartment, which took two trips each from the car to his son's apartment.

Would you believe his son never got up to help us bring in the bags? So we headed back to the house and my friend says to his son, who was still sitting on the couch playing a computer game, that next time he needed to help out. Did I mention his son is twenty-seven years old? It looked as though the young man had not washed a dish since he had moved in. On the way home, my friend told me that his son had been living there for about two years. His wife was still treating their son like a child, which made it worse.

When we left the apartment, the young man never even said thank you to his father. Here is a man who will become dependent on the care of women for the rest of his life. Mothers, teach your young men old-fashioned values. Teach them how to take care of themselves—cooking, cleaning, everything my grandmother made my brothers and I do so that we were able to take care of ourselves when we left home. Today there are a lot of young people who don't have the discipline it's going to take to survive in today's world.

## Fathers, Teach Your Daughters to Change a Flat Tire

My granddaughter and her little friend wanted me to teach them how to drive. "Not a problem," I told them.

The next day, we jumped into my car and drove out to the interstate. Then I pulled over and made them both get out of the car. I told them both that this was their first lesson in learning the ins and outs of driving, and that was by first changing a tire. You should have been there—you would have thought I asked them to walk home from the looks on their faces.

Most men know where this is going. You see, before you teach your child how to drive away from home, teach them how to get back home first. "Why can't we do this at home in the driveway?" they asked. I told them, "Because when you have a flat tire, it won't be in the driveway." The moral of this story is that dads need to teach their daughters that they don't always need a man around.

## Family Value #9

# Stages of the Family Cycle

It is just as important to understand the family life cycle as it is to understand your family history. But what is the family cycle? The family cycle is the emotional stages we all pass through from childhood into adulthood.

The stages of the family cycle are independence, marriage, parenting, launching adult children, and retirement. Each family will approach this transition differently. The transition of the family cycle is of my own opinion. Let's ask ourselves first what the family cycle is. We all know that it's the series of stages in life that our families grow through. You have heard that old saying, "It's the cycle of life." Something dies so something can live.

I have no idea who coined that statement, but I say that leans more toward the animal kingdom. But for family, it's when a person enters into the independent stages of life. We all were young teenagers and school-age kids once, and as we grow and get older, we all enter a different phase in our lives.

The family cycle is nothing more than a series of developmental stages that all families go through over time. The first family cycle is independence: *the ability to depend on one's own judgment in getting things done in order to meet their own needs.*

Second, I believe, is marriage, or working with commitment and the understanding that they are no longer one, but now have a commitment to another and their relationship. Third is parenting. As a single parent myself, I believe my experience can be valuable to you.

When it comes to parenting, remember your child or children won't always respond to what you ask or tell them to do, so when it comes time for disciplining that child, you have to be firm. At the same time, you have to be fair. A child should always know that there will be consequences for their actions. *In this family cycle, the parent is responsible for teaching the child life lessons such as accountability, responsibility, and respect. These were my most important learning tools for my son to have and take with him on his lifelong learning cycle.*

Fourth is launching adult children. After graduation from high school, my son joined the US Air Force. After four years of honorable service, he returned home to civilian life but remained in the air force reserve. He moved back in to our home to kick-start his career and college life.

Now in anyone's home, living with an adult child can be somewhat stressful. Trust me, I know. It was just my son and me, but in some homes with both parents and other younger siblings this could be a major source of tension. How did I counteract this in my house? I set very clear rules for both my son and myself.

**Note:** I said for both me and my son—he was to help by contributing to the household expenses. When dealing with your adult children who are living at home, you must create a completely new game plan for your household.

1. Set clear timelines and rules.
2. Set some financial guidelines and boundaries for the household.
3. Create a free "no judgment zone." Respect your adult child's independence without judgment.

Some of you may not agree with you adult child's choices when it comes to their careers and personal lifestyle. Living under the same roof, you all have to work together in order to live together. But once you put your ground rules into place, be sure to enforce them. When your adult child is living at home and trying to build their career, it could, in some cases, be good for their future.

The fifth family cycle, in my opinion, is probably the most important of all: retirement. For as long as I can remember when I was a young boy growing up, the retirement age in the United States was sixty-five. I remember hearing my father talking about it with some of his friends as they sat around outside playing cards, smoking, and drinking, talking about that day when they would retire and travel across the United States. You remember your Dad and Mom talking like that. Unfortunately, my father left this life at age sixty-two.

Social security benefits play an important part in the lives of most Americans. But all have seen the slow rise and change in the retirement age over the years from sixty-five, according to a University of Michigan health and retirement study.[xlvi] The Social Security Administration moved the retirement age for everyone born after 1960 up to the age of sixty-seven years old. I personally think that when it comes to preparing for our retirement, too many of us think more about getting wealthy than we do about paying off our debt.

This is a cycle of family life that is too often repeated throughout many family cultures. I created a plan that works for my home, and I'm sure anyone can. My advice to anyone when it comes to that retirement cycle is to seek out a financial adviser. Before using a financial adviser, my advice is to get some recommendations—more than two. Not being prepared for retirement, in my opinion, is the worst stage of all the family cycles.

As families, we need to look to God for help and guidance. God will help the families by the means of the wholesome values found in those families. Peer pressure at school and the winning morality in the world exert a powerful influence on the families. Love is long suffering and kind. Love is not jealous, it does not brag, and it does not get puffed up.

I, for one, can say firsthand that it is not always easy to live by the Bible's standards, but the results are well worth the effort! It has been said time and time again that there is no formula for success, but the developmental steps we all need to go through as a family affect our values. During the times of slavery, the families of African Americans were torn apart and both children and their parents were sold, separated, and taken to various geographical areas. Many of these families vowed to find their lost family members. By the end of slavery, most families had saved their money and made plans to find their loved ones and buy them and their freedom back.

But when we talk about the family cycle, we are talking family matters. No, not the television show, but like the television show, family ties are strengthened by a strong reliance on the parents, grandparents, children, and in-laws to help each other and provide the emotional and financial support of and for each family. During these times and even in my early childhood, multiple family members frequently lived in the same house, and the children learned to respect and care for each other as well as their elders.

But let's take a look on the inside of the stages of the family life cycle. I have determined that the most important stages in our family cycle are the five stages I have listed below. Now, this is only my opinion. They are listed in the order of imprints the way I see it in regard to family relationships.

**Denial:** The first reaction to any family's uncertainty is the denial of it. At the time of death or the loss of anything that the family may have cherished—home, job, you get the point—denial becomes the mechanism for defense that helps block the stages of emotion and the pain of loss. In other words, being in a state of denial is nothing more than an act of keeping yourself from the reality of your situation.

**Anger:** Anger is nothing more than inner pain emerging and the reality of its emotions being expressed over the loss. When we talk about emotions, I believe anger is the most powerful emotion one can experience when they are upset with someone or mad about something.

**Depression:** Depression is the reaction related to a loss, regret, sadness, and isolation. I have listened to lots of people who are in this stage, and they talk about not spending enough time with the ones who have passed on or how much more they could have done to keep from losing their home. I have determined that depression has more of a connection to a person experiencing loss. At some time in our lives, we all have lost interest in something we cared about at one time. After my combat duty in Vietnam, I suffered from depression and post-traumatic stress disorder (PTSD). We all have been irritable and upset, but depression is a little different from the others, and it can affect anyone. Depression is a serious but common problem that affects every family in a different way.

**Grieving:** When we lose a loved one or when we lose anything of value, we all go through a period of grieving. There are different types of grief, and it's important to understand that grieving is a part of life's process. There's a time for grieving and a time to move on and live your life. I lost my older brother in 1994. I thought at that time it was the most significant loss of my life. I loved my older brother, and here recently I lost my younger brother to the court system. The loss of both my brothers is a grieving experience unimaginable and uncontrollable for me. Everyone works through their grief differently. What this means is that each person's physical, emotional, and psychological feelings, including the spiritual, can be overwhelming—I know it was and still is for me. There are factors that relate to grief, like your feelings toward the person who died, and if there's a support system for you. But when you can get that reassurance and the feeling of being understood, the recovery process will begin to complete itself.

**Acceptance**: In the family cycle, acceptance is understanding the different perspectives of the family cycle, being aware and acknowledging your own self-acceptance and behavior. Real quick, on the subject of acceptance, let's get a good understanding of it. We are not talking about that high school "accept me" into that female, territorial cheerleader club. What I'm talking about is the challenges that life will present us on a day-to-day basis and having the willingness to accept it and work through it instead of resisting it. In our life, we all want some things to work out differently, but at this moment in time, you, me, them, all of us need to accept things as they are until we can develop that positive attitude and mindset to accept and embrace whatever comes our way.

## Family Value #10

# The Military Family

One thing for sure is that the military is committed to the families' well-being and provides readiness support groups to assist the families of military personnel. It has been reported that 70 percent of military families have adjusted well to the demands of being a military family.[xlvii] It works to give families the support they need for their quality of life. It also helps to manage the normal family stress and the challenges of military life that come with it.

I come to you on this subject as a military person who lived through all the adjustments a military family has to make. All children have the right to a healthy lifestyle and the right to also experience a strong family life that helps the military-service member stay committed to the military. But violence can affect any family when stress builds up. When violence is part of a military family's lifestyle, it affects everyone, including the spouse, the children, the service member, and their command.

All families have and will face some type of stress, such as being newly married or having financial troubles. In this case, both spouses need to make adjustments as they start building their lives together, and come up with a plan on meeting their major expenses, credit-card spending, and balancing a checkbook. These qualities can help any family stay strong and work together in their times of stress.

## Dealing with Deployments

The military is always ready to help its servicemen and servicewomen build a healthy lifestyle together. But being in the military sometimes means having to face deployment and transfer issues that the nonmilitary family may never face. When you have good communication, it will help with misunderstandings about the separations.

Conflict and misunderstanding are a normal part of life, but not knowing how to handle conflict will make it difficult to find a solution toward a peaceful end. According to Military.com and the *Military Times*, the percentage of military personnel staying in until retirement has increased 60 percent. The opportunity for young men and women to serve their country and develop job skills has increased 80 percent. [xlvii]

## Some Facts about Military Families

According to a November 2012 report by the Pew Research Center Social & Demographic Trends and Veterans Survey, over half the men and women who fight to keep freedom alive in this country have a spouse and children. Most of us don't know this, but women make up 95 percent of military spouses, and 80 percent are thirty-five years or younger. One in ten active-duty members are married, and their spouses are in the military as well. (But our military children are at a higher risk of developing aggressive behavior.) Eighty-three percent of Vietnam combat veterans' children have a higher aggression score than children of nonveterans.

## Family Value #11

# Who's Raising Our Sons to be Fathers?

*"The real man stands up to his responsibilities and provides his family with what they deserve."*

—Carlton Young, PhD

The family image is ever changing, and I have to ask what's next. Growing up back in my day, it didn't take much for a young man to know when he had to display respect not only to his mother and father, but to adults in general. Most of that came from the fact that, back then, most families had both parents in the home. Most of you who are reading this book remember the musical group Smokey Robinson and the Miracles. I think it was about early to mid-1970s when he wrote the lyrics, "My daughter is going to have a baby, and she's only a baby herself." I remember standing in my living room, holding my daughter, my firstborn, and thinking to myself, *No matter what takes place, I will always be in your life.*

As I look back at the '70s and '80s, I see that there has been an increase in the single-family home. So when we talk about and see the disrespect our children have in the hallways of our schools, I can't help but believe that is due to the fact that our family structure has collapsed. Our fathers are disappearing from the households, and most mothers are not old enough to care for themselves, let alone care for a small child. I was visiting my granddaughter's high school during the week that all the seniors were preparing for their graduation. I went into the school auditorium, where some of the high school seniors were asked to come up and say something about their parents. If there were one hundred students that came to the front of the auditorium, I would have to say 63 percent of the students that came up front came from a single-family home. It was like three out of every four students referred to the one parent as “my mom has been with me and my brothers/sisters ever since,” indicating they were part of a single-family home.

I would often visit the high school, and last year I helped with the training of their high school’s JROTC program. But there was just one thing that really bothered me about the young men and women at the school—that most, in my opinion, had no respect for the teachers, their school, for each other, or for themselves.

I think it is just unacceptable how young men today have their pants sagging below their underclothing. The young women aren’t doing much better. Our young men are on a dangerous spiral, a spiral that indicates that our young men will father children and, at some early stage, walk out of their child’s life.

## Just Like Your No-Good Daddy

I was in the mall last Christmas, and just like the rest of us, I got a little irritated during that time of the season. But I saw something that just told me that times had changed, and young mothers—not all, but there’s a lot—trying to raise young boys are not capable of doing it; well, at least not on their own.

What makes me say this? There was a young mother walking through the mall with her young son, who was asking for everything he laid his eyes on, something we all expect as parents. But here is what took place. The boy was about six or seven years old; the mother about twenty-four or twenty-five years old. I could tell her education was very limited by the way she spoke to her child and with the other young lady who was shopping with her.

The young boy kept asking for toy after toy nonstop, to the point that the young mother lashed out, grabbing the young boy and shouting, “Shut the f— up!” As she raised her hand as if she were going to slap him in the mouth. “You’re just like your no-good daddy!” she shouted at the young boy.

Have we stopped to think that our children will replay whatever image we place in front of them? Let’s take a closer look at this and see if we can get a better understanding. Mothers, if you are living with a man who is abusive both verbally and physically, and you are not making any efforts to get out of that relationship, you need to understand that you are in danger not just for your life, but of acting out your own anger and aggression toward your child. The circumstances in which verbal abuse takes place can make a big difference in how your child will respond.

Example: you're in a relationship where there is abuse. You're being physically, emotionally, and verbally abused, and like a lot of young mothers, you allow the father/boyfriend/husband to continue the abuse that your young male child sees on a daily basis. What do you think the child's reaction is going to be when he reaches the age of young adulthood and you keep telling him he's just like his no-good daddy? It's going to be exactly what you have been receiving from his father.

If the baby's daddy has been going upside your head, what do you think the words "just like your no-good daddy" are telling your young man? They're telling him to do unto you and other women as your husband/boyfriend/his father does unto you. Don't believe it? Keep telling him those words. In the book *Psycho-Cybernetics*, published in 2001 by Prentice Hall Press, New York, New York, by Maxwell Maltz, M.D., F.I.C.S., it said that your mind doesn't know what's real and what's imagined. Whatever you feed it, eventually it will believe.

For every statistic, for every story told, there's a face someone knows. I've been asked millions of times by parents, "Where did we lose our kids?" My answer is always the same: we lost our children to a second-rate educational system and the lack of social and family leadership. There are not enough, if any, positive, empowering life-skill programs being presented to our youth in today's schools. The biggest thing we as parents need to be concerned about is the crisis our children face day to day.

But here's your fly in the ointment, your monkey in the wrench: The crisis our youth face today does not greet them when they enter the doors of our educational institutions, nor does a crisis embrace them in our penal institutions. Their crisis doesn't start when they drop out of school. The crisis our children are facing begins long before they begin school and long after they drop out—it begins at home. And we wonder why our young black men have low levels of self-esteem.

## The Communication Mechanisms: One Man's Opinion

I'm an old-fashioned kind of guy who believes in the world of communication. No, not the World Wide Web or the Internet. I'm talking one-on-one, old-fashioned communication. Communication is the buzzword that families need to bring back to the table. The young generation today, believe it or not, is starving for some real communication skills. Unfortunately, the household is incapable of communicating to our children. Why? Most parents are unable to communicate with each other, let alone with their children.

Walking the halls of our high schools, I can see from the actions of our young men and women they are hungry for attention, love, and positive conversation from us, the parents, the teachers, the adults. But how do we communicate to this young generation? How do we feed their hunger? What should our conversations be about when talking to our youth?

For starters, we as adults should talk to our young men about what they think is standing in the way of their education and academic success. I'm going to go out on a limb here and voice my opinion on what I think is holding our young men back and making them lousy fathers and terrible husbands for our daughters.

Here's my belief: first, let me start with the rap culture. When I hear the type of music that is being promoted to our young men, it's my belief this form of music is a mind-altering guide that is leading our young black men to a life of crime on the streets, not worrying about the outcome, the aftereffect, the consequences of their actions, nor their education. Right about now, some of you are hopping mad about what I just said about rap music and its culture. But I never said that all rap music and everything about the culture is bad; it's not. Two schools of thought here: My ex-wife's son, my stepson, listened to rap music and sagged his jeans, but he allowed that culture to overtake him. Coupled with the fact I was never allowed to discipline him for his bad behavior, his actions overtook him and he is now a three-time felon.

On the other hand, my youngest son, whom I raised as a single parent, listened to the same rap music, but I regulated his usage, did not allow him to sag, and school and homework were first priority. Today, he's a successful businessman with a large corporation. I'm convinced that this can happen in anyone's home, be they single- or two-parent homes.

## Things

Take a good look at your children. Are you really in touch with what they are wearing? I recall my daughter telling me she wanted to go live with her mother in California. When I asked her reason for wanting to go, she said, "Because she will buy me things."

What our children see in the malls and on display, they want. They have no idea of cost or what it takes for the parent to be able to give them what they want. Shoes and clothes have become more important to our children than their education. We live in a fast-moving world today, so fast that most parents can't keep up. Technology is an ever-changing "thing." It's all around us, day in and day out. We went from rotary phones to cell phones, and now we have smartphones.

Mom and Dad can't compete with technology, drugs, and fast cars. Education is out, and respect is something of the past. Everything good is out and everything bad is in. Our daughters are becoming bum magnets, and our young men are becoming more and more disrespectful toward our young daughters, and they are doing it in public to the point it's becoming the thing to do to call a young woman a bitch or ho. But what bothers me the most is that there are a lot of parents who allow their sons and daughters to conduct themselves without respect for authority.

I have seen this in our own schools and on the streets of our own communities. Now, this is what's going to get your daughters pregnant, but don't worry, there won't be a committed relationship because these are the young men who are not well educated and don't know or understand the meaning of the word *responsibility*. These are the young men who have no respect for their own mothers, so why would you think they would have respect for your daughters?

## What's Missing

We need to implement life-skills mentorships into our school systems. How do we get something like this started, and how do we mentor our young people? First, we need to put our young people in front of the people who are able to empower them to tap into and maximize their own potential, and this needs to be done one person at a time. We need to educate our young people on the fact that life is interested in results! The big question for our young men and women on that day they become adults will not be "What do you know?" but rather "What will you do with what you know?"

Please, let's not allow our young people to set themselves up for failure by depriving them of the resources for their personal growth. Let's educate and invest in the school, the teachers, and most of all, the lives of our children.

## Family Value #12

# Real People, Real Letters, Real Advice

Below is a collection of letters that I've received from people asking for my help in dealing with dilemmas in their lives. I felt it was very important for me to include these letters and my responses because of the many readers who also may be facing some of the same challenges.

---

*Dear America's Grandfather,*

*I just found out that I am HIV positive. I am twenty years old and a gay man. I am a college student, and I have not told my parents yet. My parents don't even know that I am gay. How do I tell them? My father is a pastor and my mom is a community leader. Both of them don't support gay people, and my dad always talks about what the Bible says about homosexuality. I am scared. I have thought about suicide.*

*Help me please!*
*Jimmy J.*

*Dear Jimmy J.,*

*First, let me start at the end of your letter. You need to know from the top that suicide is a permanent solution to a temporary problem. Here's a quote I wrote for people just like you: "It's a weak man who has to sell drugs, pimp women, and do something illegal to make a living because he thinks he can't find a job. But it's a straight-up coward who would take their own life because they didn't have the courage to face the challenges that life has to offer."*

*You have heard the old saying "the elephant in the room"? I hope I can help you understand the dynamics of what you are asking by asking you a probing question. Have you told your partner about being HIV positive? It sounds as though you have bigger problems than your parents finding out you are gay.*

*Second, it sounds as though you are suffering from the struggle of accommodating your parents about your homosexuality. Jimmy, if you are going to live the life regardless of what your parents may think and what God has to say about it, you have to man up. You are a grown man, and you should not only be responsible for your actions, but your first responsibility is to your partner. Suicide is not it! Man up and face the elephant in the room. Talk with your parents and talk with God.*

*Sincerely,*
*America's Grandfather*

***

*Dear America's Grandfather,*

*I recently lost my job and my health insurance coverage. I am married with three kids, all under twelve years old. My oldest son needs ongoing medical care. I don't know where to turn to or how to take care of my family. We are three months behind on the rent, the car needs to be repaired, and I am at my wit's end.*

*I need a strong shoulder to lean on right now. I try to keep a smile on my face for the family, but it is getting hard. Any suggestions would help me to keep on keeping on.*

*Joe*

*Dear Joe,*

*Let's think about the day you graduated from college and took that great job that helped you and your family do all the things you dreamed of. Do you remember that? You went out into the world with confidence, and you were energized with a purpose to make a difference. Now you lost your job and your health insurance coverage and you think you don't have a purpose anymore. Read about King Solomon; he gathered enormous wealth and pursued pleasure, but found that those things brought no lasting sense of purpose. What you are feeling is a loss of purpose. Joe, no one loses purpose in life; they give it away. You lost your job, not your balls. Get creative and start your own thing. What was it you did for the company you used to work for? Take that skill and create your own business.*

*I had to do that myself. I believe that those who study and apply what they learn find that their life changes for the better. You gain the conviction that your life has real purpose when you get creative. So get creative, Joe. You have not lost a thing. Let me leave you with the words of Les Brown, world-renowned motivational speaker, and a dear friend of mine: "When life knocks you down, land on your back, because if you can look up, you can get up!"*

*Get Up!*
*America's Grandfather*

***

*Dear America's Grandfather,*

*We buried our grandmother last month. She was the rock of our family. My three sisters are now fighting over her estate and destroying the family because of greed. What would you tell them and the family to save peace?*

*Louise*

*Dear Louise,*

*The more I read these letters, the more I have flashbacks. I lost my mother in 2006, and my three sisters worked real hard to push me out so they could keep the family estate for themselves. What you are seeing is the breakdown, the loss of respect and dignity between themselves. Don't get involved to the point where you become a part of the same.*

*When the probate courts step in, there won't be much to fight over. Trust me, I've been there. You need to be the sole foundation of what is left of your family and not worry about the outcome of the estate.*

*One thing you can do, as I did and still do, is to forgive your sisters, pray, and let God handle everything else. Don't be concerned about what's going on with your sisters. Be concerned with the rest of your family. To this day, my sisters and I don't speak, so I love them from a distance. Don't stop loving your family.*

*This too will pass!*
*America's Grandfather*

***

*Dear America's Grandfather,*

*I am in a wheelchair due to a bad car accident, and I am twenty-nine years old. I have no friends and no family to help me or even visit me to give me someone to talk to. I have decided that you will become my grandfather. Thank you for being there for me and millions of others who need an elder to look up to. I am trying to stay positive and keep my head up, but sometimes, I just want someone to show me that they care about me.*

*Lacey*

*Dear Lacey,*

*I am the grandfather to America, and I try to give the best advice I know how, but one thing about me is I will not BS you. I will tell you what you need to hear. Don't dwell on your disability or how it happened.*

*I will be here for you if you need advice and someone to talk to about what's going on in your life. I encourage you to read my books, listen to my CDs, and if you can, come to some of my workshops and presentations. I'm sure you will get what you are looking to achieve.*

*Sincerely,*
*America's Grandfather*

***

*Dear America's Grandfather,*

*I am a doctor in an urban clinic and I see so many black people who are sick because of a lack of healthy eating and exercise. I wish there were a way that we could stress the importance of taking care of our bodies to a generation of people who really don't take health seriously. As a wise man, what is your message to the community about healthy living?*

*Dr. Ty*

*Dear Dr. Ty,*

*Wow! This is something that we have overlooked for the better part of our lives. When you talk about informing our communities on healthier living, I would say that we as community leaders, educators, and concerned parents need to be more of an example to our families and our communities. But good health is not just about eating healthy or getting out and exercising on a daily and weekly basis. I think we all have dropped the ball in this department of life. We need to keep in mind that good health is also having a healthy, positive mental attitude.*

*I would think my message to the community and its families would be that we all need to exercise more and eat more fruits and vegetables. We should also cut down on the processed foods we eat and drink more water. Another wise thing is to contact our local and community leaders and demand their support for recommendations and access to a plan of action to identify the needs to build a healthier community.*

*Live healthy!*
*America's Grandfather*

***

*Dear America's Grandfather,*

*I'm a sixty-year-old grandmother with ten grandkids who all live with me. My daughters are not fit to be mothers, and two of them are in prison. I am tired of being a full-time mother. I have raised my own children and I want to go out and live my life. I am still young-looking and I want to date, I want to travel, and I want my house back.*

*I love all of my grandbabies, but I am tired and I want out. How can I get out of this mess? I have prayed and prayed, but every day I see my attitude getting worse and the kids even see the change. I don't want to cook or clean. This is not me. I need some advice. Can you help me resolve this issue?*

*Also, the kids' fathers are not involved, nor do they want to be in anyway. I do get money, but not enough.*

*Ms. Lois*

*Dear Ms. Lois,*

*I understand where you are coming from; there was a time when I was raising my granddaughter. It was only for a brief time, but I learned so much. Grandparents are caring for their grandkids more these days than ever before.*

*What we have here is called a generational gap, when the parents of our grandkids can't hold up their responsibility. Reading your letter, it sounds as though you want to stop being a grandparent. You can't allow your attitude to get in the way of the care of the children.*

*At this point, you are asking yourself where you went wrong. Don't start blaming yourself for the shortcomings of someone else. You have not lost your home; it's still yours, and you still have a life. And at sixty years young, I'm sure you are a great-looking lady. Your life at this point has been thrown off balance. Here is what you can do.*

*In my experience, the grandparents are committed to the care of the grandchild. What you may need to do is look into financial assistance that may be available for grandparents raising grandchildren. Look into the agency on aging, the AARP Grandparent Information Center, at 888-OUR-AARP (697-2277) or www.aarp.org/grandparents.*

*In some states, child support payments may be transferred to you if the father is paying child support. You will need to submit an application with the Office of the Attorney General (800-252-8014) and they can help. Your life is not over; it has just begun. There is so much information out there for grandparents caring for their grandchildren that once you tap into it, it will change your situation. Depending on your income, childcare can be available through Child Care Group programs.*

*My very best to you,*
*America's Grandfather*

***

*Dear America's Grandfather,*

*I am an eighteen-year-old male who is homeless. My parents put me out when they found out that I'm gay. I am now living with whoever will take me in. There have been many nights that I slept in the park or just walked all night long with no place to go. I am scared, and I don't know what to do. I want to go home, but my dad has threatened to kill me because of being gay. I could tell him that I am not gay and he would let me come back home, but I would be lying and it would catch up with me. What do you think I should do?*

*Gay Male*

*My dear friend,*

*I have talked to so many young men and women in your position who have wondered about this same question for a long time. I am going to tell you some things that may not change the outlook of your relationship with your family, but it will ease some of the tension.*

*Your father is not going to kill you if you go back home and talk with him. Your father doesn't hate you; what he hates is the fear and prejudice that have been placed on the gay community. Most straight men I have talked with who say they hate gays only feel that way because they are not secure with their own sexuality. Your father is working off the fear, prejudice, hate, and dislike of gays because he's afraid someone will accuse him of being gay as well.*

*People fear what they don't understand. What they don't understand is the elephant in the room, and no one is talking about it. It has been said that education could solve the problem, but what is the problem: you being gay, or me being afraid of gays? You didn't tell your father anything that he has not had suspicions about for a while, but you coming out and telling him threw him for a loop.*

*"Let me be suspicious—just never tell me the truth." I coined this motto about three years ago after having a talk with some fathers that said their sons or daughters were gay.*

*Here in Atlanta about six to eight months ago, we had a gay bashing, if you will. A young man was jumped by a group of young men because he was gay. It's not because one is gay—I don't believe anyone has a problem with that—it's the way you carry yourself. That's why I believe heterosexual men have a problem with homosexual men.*

*My advice to is to visit www.PFLAG.org, a national voluntary organization dedicated to supporting parents and their lesbian, gay, and bisexual daughters and sons.*

*We all have to come together against the discrimination and for the rights of others. The fight starts with understanding, love, and education. Your father can change locks on the doors, he can change the home address, he can change just about anything, but he can't change the fact you are his son.*

*Good luck!*
*America's Grandfather*

***

*Dear America's Grandfather,*

*I am writing you from prison. I am doing ten to fifteen years for a stupid crime I committed when I was a teenager. I need to make something of my life now. I am twenty-three years old and working on my GED while being locked up. I never had a relationship with my dad or any male. I was raised by my older sister, who did the best she could with a hardheaded young boy like I was. My question to you is, What advice can you give me to help me prepare mentally to come out of here and start my life all over again?*

*Thank you for your time,*
*Mitch*

*Dear Mitch,*

*I don't know how much longer you have to be there, or how old you were when you went into prison, but reading that you are working on your GED is a good start to a better life after you get out. Here is what I recommend you do. You spoke of your sister raising you, but you were hardheaded, so that tells me you were unable to follow her directions.*

*Mitch, sit down and write your sister a letter apologizing for your actions and asking for her forgiveness. This may open the doors of communication between you and your sister, something you need to do long before you leave prison. Many men and women find themselves homeless after being released from prison, and single people like yourself are particularly at risk. Now is the time for you to start looking into housing programs for ex-offenders.*

*Don't let the GED be the only education you give yourself. Start looking into trade schools, find out who your probation officer might be, and start talking with him/her about your future. If you are unable to go back to your sister's home, don't get frustrated with her; try to understand her side. But all is not lost; the probation services will help you find housing and employment. But the better you prepare yourself during the time you are still in prison, the better you will be prepared when you get out. Your future is in your hands, and only you can control that. Let me leave you with this quote. Write it down—put it up someplace where you can see it and read it daily.*

*"Show me your friends and I'll show you your future."*

*—John Kuebler*
*Wishing you the best,*
*America's Grandfather*

***

*Dear America's Grandfather,*

*I am getting out of the United States Air Force in a few months. What should I do next with my life? I am confused with what my life is about. I want to start a church, but don't know how to do that. I know that God is using me to help others. Any advice for me?*

*Walter, SSGT*

*Dear SSGT Walter,*

*Out of all the letters I have answered to my readers, yours is probably one of the easiest ones I have read. You don't have a problem, and there is no reason for you to be confused. Everything you need to know about your next life is right in front of you.*

*Here is what I think you should do if you are truly serious about starting a church. You might want to take a good look at the chaplain services before getting out of the USAF. They have a great program that someone like you would benefit from.*

*Too often, young men like yourself are quick to leave the military to pursue a new career and don't know anything about their new career. I had a friend that did just what I am suggesting to you. He became an air force chaplain and later retired as a major and started his own church in Oklahoma City. Use the resources at hand, or at least check them out first before you get out. Above all, pray about what God would have you do.*

*Encouragement,*
*America's Grandfather*

***

*Dear America's Grandfather,*

*I am a single father raising twin daughters. My daughters just turned thirteen, and they are getting out of control. One of them was in a fight at school and got suspended. The other one is acting out and causing me a lot of stress. Their mother died in a car accident about a year ago, and I am doing my best to be both Mom and Dad.*

*I work a lot so I can maintain a roof over our heads. I have no family in Atlanta where we live, so I am going crazy trying to be a full-time dad and at the same time have a life. I think the loss of their mother is causing them to act out. They were close to their mom, and the loss in all of our lives is painful. There have been many nights when I just cry in my room and ask God to help me go on.*

*I don't know what to do. I need your help to tell me something to save my girls and my own sanity.*

*Joe*

*Dear Joe,*

*First, let me extend to you my deepest sympathy on the passing of your wife and the mother of your two daughters. I myself was a single father, but through divorce. I was left to raise my daughter and son on my own. My son never gave me any real problems, but my daughter was a completely different story. She gave grief from every angle you could imagine.*

*Your daughters are not, in a sense, acting out. They really miss their mother. You might want to look at the time you are spending away from home working. The problem is not your daughters, it's your time. Your job is not going anywhere, but if you don't stop and take the time out to reconnect with your daughters and rebuild your lives as a family, you are looking at more grief and stress as time goes on.*

*You were a full-time dad before their mother passed away, so why is trying to be a full-time dad now driving you crazy? Let me say this to you: Reach down and grab hold of them, and stand up and continue being the father that you have always been. Surround yourself with your daughters and the pleasant memories of your wife, their mother. Go visit family. You have the rest of your life to start over. For now, trying to have a life outside of being a full-time dad might be a little premature at this early stage in the loss of your wife and in the lives of your daughters.*

*Joe, your daughters are not acting out, they're reaching out to you as their father. They were close to their mother; bring them closer to you.*

*Blessing to you and yours,*
*America's Grandfather*

***

*Dear America's Grandfather,*

*How are you today? What has been your experience in dealing with decisions on how to retire and enjoy life? I am sixty-three years old and I want to retire, but I have no savings. I don't own my home and I need to work. I am depressed. I screwed up my life a long time ago, and now I am paying for it.*

*Please give me something to guide me through this last phase of my life.*

*Leon*

*Dear Leon,*

*Let me put it to you like this. First, you need to stop making excuses for your mistakes—no joke! As long as you are complaining about what you did wrong, you will never get started on doing it right. Looking around, who are you surrounding yourself with?*

*At sixty-three, you are past due for purging yourself of your dead weight. That dead weight is the people in your life who aren't going anywhere and are keeping you from doing the same. This is to include family members. The thing about it is, Leon, you know who they are, and it's time to drop them from your life.*

*When you talk about not owning your home, look at your timeline (your age). At this point in life, you need to focus on getting a place that you can afford in the event you never own a home. But that's okay, you are not alone. There are millions of people younger than you and in your age group who have never owned their own home.*

*Don't be depressed. I'm here to tell you that you have not screwed up your life; you have found ways not to do what you have been doing. In other words, you know what it's going to take to fail and what it's going to take to succeed in your new life. This is not the last phase of your life. Remember and live by the following quote:*

*"Failure is a success if we learn from it."*

*—Malcolm Forbes*
*No more excuses!*
*America's Grandfather*

***

*Dear Grandfather,*

*I want to know if you will loan me $10,000 so I can buy a car. My mom is a single mother and not working. If I could buy a car, I could get a job and help out with the food and other expenses. I have nowhere else to turn to, and since you are our "grandfather," I was told that is what you do. If you can do this for me, I will pay you back one day.*

*Thanks,*
*Mike, nineteen years old*

*Dear Mike,*

*Great way to start out asking for money, and the amount is not bad. Here's my problem, Mike: We don't even know each other, and you come right out asking me for $10,000 for a car. Well, Mike, you can get a great, running starter car for $2,000. I know because I just helped my granddaughter get one for college. You say you want to help your mother with food and other expenses.*

*Well, you asked me for my advice, so here it is: you are nineteen years old, young, and strong as an ox. You can join the military, get a great job, have an income that will help you buy a car, and help out at home. In some cases in the military, you might be able to make your mother your dependent, enabling her to get a military ID and have access to the military bases.*

*But in your case, here is what I have come up with. I try to give advice to families and young people all around the country. I have read more letters than you can imagine. After reading yours, I went back more than twenty years in the marine corps and came up with this: You are trying to bullshit the bullshitter and snow the snowman. Been there, done that. When you have real problems, real questions, and would like real advice, write back.*

*Can't help you!*
*America's Grandfather*

# Letters of Praise

## for America's Grandfather and *Family Values*

*Dr. Young, I will always remember your willingness to work with our son and tutor him in the ASVAB so that he could get into the army. You worked with him for right at a year, and when he took the test the first time, he passed with a score of forty-nine. Thank you for your time and your heartfelt concern for our son.*

—Mr. and Mrs. Darius Mitchell
Parents of Brandon

*Dr. Young, thank you for all you do and for what you have done for both my sons. You have worked with them from ages six and ten to sixteen and twenty. You were the one who taught them how to tie a tie and helped teach them how to drive, although my oldest took your car without your permission and almost drove it over a cliff. I had never seen such patience in a person as I saw in you. You talked to my sons with such love and concern. Today, my oldest is in his second year of college and will be graduating as an engineer from Georgia Tech, and my youngest is doing outstanding in school because of your adult and loving, father-type leadership to them both, and your commitment to the youth in our community.*

—Dr. Carla Atkins
Educator

*After the death of my husband, my son had the hardest time dealing with it. His grades dropped in school, and he all but gave up. Raising him became more difficult as time passed. Dr. Young mentored my son for about a year, and through his workshops, my son was inspired to complete his education and is now pursuing a career in the US Army.*

—Ms. Andrea Willis
Single Parent/Nursing Administrator

*The hardest job I ever had was raising my granddaughter at age sixty-eight, and she had started to lose sight of everything I was trying to teach her. It's not easy being sixty-eight when the child is eighteen. But thanks to Dr. Young for stepping in. His advice and his mentoring of my granddaughter made a big difference in her attitude. Because of the time Dr. Young took to work with her, she is now a more positive, stronger, and more focused young woman, and is working on a great career for her. Thank you, Dr. Young.*

—Ms. Jera Jones
Grandmother

A Grandfather's
Prayer for Family Wisdom
*Father, I thank you that the communication of my faith becomes effectual by acknowledging every good thing which is in me, Christ Jesus. I hear the voice of the Good Shepherd. I hear my Father's voice, and the voice of a stranger I will not follow. Father, I believe in my heart and say with my mouth that this day, the will of God is done in my life. I walk in a manner worthy of you, Lord, fully pleasing to you and desiring to please you in all things, bearing fruit in every good work. Jesus has been made unto me wisdom. I single-mindedly walk in that wisdom, expecting to know what to do in every situation and to be on top of every circumstance!*
*In Jesus's name, amen!*

My blessing to all,
America's Grandfather

This prayer is from *Prayers That Avail Much,* Volume One, World Ministries, Inc.

# The Ten Dos and Don'ts
## of America's Grandfather
## for Living and Overcoming Family Crisis

The Ten Don'ts of America's Grandfather

How many times have you heard people say, "You don't know what I've been through or what I'm going through in my life!" I would like to give you my ten don'ts to surviving a crisis. Add your own personal comments to the don'ts in your relationship.

10. Don't try to change him/her; appreciate them for who they are right now.

______________________________________________

______________________________________________

______________________________________________

______________________________________________

______________________________________________

9. Don't violate each other's privacy.

______________________________________________

______________________________________________

______________________________________________

______________________________________________

______________________________________________

8. Don't compare each other to fictional characters you've seen in the movies.

______________________________________________

______________________________________________

______________________________________________

______________________________________________

______________________________________________

7. Don't withhold sex as a weapon for punishment of bad behavior or use it as a reward for good behavior.

6. Don't talk to your partner as if they were a child.

5. Don't criticize or put each other down in front of family and friends.

4. Don't give in to what is perceived to be a lopsided relationship.

3. Don't attempt to talk to your partner during a movie or at a sporting event.

2. Don't keep insisting that your partner needs to share their feelings.

1. Don't ever go to bed angry.

## THE 10 DOS OF AMERICA'S GRANDFATHER

All relationships are like being at Six Flags-they are one hell of a roller-coaster ride, but you do have fun! Add your comments to the following relationship.

10. Always accept your partner's “no” graciously.

9. Your partner cannot read your mind, so always ask for what you really want!

8. Always support each other!

7. Make it a point to always honor your agreements to each other!

6. Do your best to become creatively intimate as often as possible!

5. Make all your time positive quality time!

4. Always trust and respect each other!

3. Appreciate and show appreciation for the little things you do for each other!

2. Always give your partner time to do his or her own thing!

1. Stop nagging, and just talk!

# Reflections from America's Grandfather

*In the pursuit of your purpose, there are requirements we all must understand. Answer each question the way you understand your passion for your family and your life.*

Family Values Chapter #1: OLD-FASHIONED WAYS (THE FAMILY DINNER)

What are some of the traditional day-to-day challenges you have getting your family to the dinner table, and what are some of things you think you might need to change, if any?

Ways we can reclaim our family:

Teaching respect:

Creating family, pray time:

Family Values Chapter # 4: MOTHERS WHO ARE BOTH MOM AND DAD

How can I become a better single mom/dad?

Understanding Trouble: (What is it I see coming?)

Understanding Your Journey: (Where am I/are we headed?)

How well do I handle my out-of-control youth?

Are there consequences in my home?

Is my family built to last?

Who is my child hanging out with?

# Family Values #5:

# It Takes a Village to Raise a Child (A Message to Fathers)

What can I do in my village?

Is there a "real man" in the home?

My support in tough times comes from:

Section 6: FAMILY UNCERTAINTY-DEALING WITH DOUBT AND TIMES OF UNCERTAINTY

What is the uncertainty in the family?

What am I/are we doing about it?

Section 7: HEALTHY LIFESTYLE

Our family's health and lifestyle:

Section 8: FAMILY BASIC TRAINING 101

What are we doing to save our family?

THE #1 FAMILY VALUE OVER ALL
UNLEASH YOUR PASSION FOR YOUR FAMILY!

*America's Grandfather*

Contact info

To book Dr. Carlton N. Young to speak at your next event, please contact:

Bob Gaubert @ 770-267-7087 or email: bgaubert@aol.com or contact: Dr. Carlton N. Young at life@carltonyoung.com. Or call 404-212-9965/404-694 9965

www.drcarltonyoung.com

# Resources For Families Seeking Help

There are thousands of websites of organizations, faith- based groups, government departments, and social service agencies that provide families help to survive.

My top recommendations are:

## REFERENCES

- www.Military.com
- The Sloan Work and Family Reach Network
- www.thecreditsolutionprogram.com
- www.GoldSeek.com
- www.WebMD.com
- KLOGIX
- www.Helium.com
- www.Answers.com
- www.Themotherco.com
- www.Justpeace.org
- www.cancer.org
- www.disabilitycanhappen.org
- www.heart.org
- www.iamconcerned.org

## FAMILY SERVICE AGENCIES

- Center for the Visually Impaired
- Department of Health
- In-House Elderly Care Senior Living
- Bureau of Elderly and Adult Services
- Adult Protective Services

## FAITH-BASED GROUPS

- www.en.arocha.org
- www.alternatives@simpleliving.org
- www.arecology.org www.ausable.org
- www.nrpe.org
- www.interfaithpower.org
- www.billjacobs@catholic.org
- www.conservation.catholic.org
- www.newdream.org

## ADDITIONAL RESOURCES

Parke, Ross and K. Alison Clarke-Stewart. "Effects of Parental Incarceration on Young Children." Retrieved November 12, 2012. https://aspe.hhs.gov/basic-report/effects-parental-incarceration-young-children.

Wright, Lois and Cynthia Seymour. "Effects of Parental Incarceration on Children and Families." Accessed November 12, 2012. http://www.familyimpactseminars.org/s_mifis05c03.pdf (page discontinued).

Chronus Corporation. Accessed April 6, 2016. www.chronus.com.

Volunteer Match. Accessed April 6, 2016. www.VolunteerMatch.org.

Griffin, Marlene. References for Dos and Don'ts.

WomenOver40Health.com

# About The Author

Dr. Carlton N. Young is known for his dynamic, entertaining, powerful, and incredible speaking performances as a keynote motivational and inspirational speaker. Dr. Young has survived cancer, suffered from post-traumatic stress disorder (PTSD), and struggled with depression and thoughts of suicide that impaired his ability to function both socially and occupationally. Now, the "World Champion of Inspiration" and "Foremost Expert on Homelessness in America," in his personal development series Empowered to Succeed, reveals the benefits and applications of positive thinking and the power of faith. Dr. Young is the author of the critically acclaimed From Home to Homeless to Success and the best- selling Powerful Life Quotes for Success. Young competed in the Toastmasters International World Championship of Public Speaking contest as one out of 32,000 contestants from 127 countries who competed in a yearlong process of elimination. In August of 2015, Dr. Young became one of the top one hundred speakers in the world.

Dr. Young is also the coauthor of three books: Unleash the Greatness within You, Unleash the Passion for Your Purpose, and From Mediocre to Magnificent. Dr. Young has been branded as "America's Grandfather," and now his newest book, Family Values, is the first of five volumes from his Empowerment Development series.

# Endnotes

---


[i] Doherty, William and Barbara Carlson. *Putting Family First: Successful Strategies for Reclaiming Family Life in a Hurry-Up World.* New York: Holt Paperbacks, 2002.

[ii] Brooks, Carol. "What Happened When the Praying Stopped?" Inplainsite.org. http://www.inplainsite.org/what_happened_when_the_praying.html.

[iii] Washington, Jesse. "Blacks struggle with 72 percent unwed mothers rate." NBCNews.com. November 07, 2010. http://www.nbcnews.com/id/39993685/ns/health-womens_health/t/blacks-struggle-percent-unwed-mothers-rate/#.WRylpWgrKUk.

[iv] "Myth That There are More Black Men in Prison Than College is Debunked." New America Media. February 18, 2015. http://newamericamedia.org/2015/02/myth-that-there-are-more-black-men-in-prison-than-college-is-debunked.php.

[v] Desmond-Harris, Jenee. "The myth that there are more black men in prison than in college, debunked in one chart." Vox. February 12, 2015. https://www.vox.com/2015/2/12/8020959/black-men-prison-college.

[vi] Buckner, Jerry L. "Black Males: An Endangered Species." Contending for the Faith. http://sites.silaspartners.com/partner/Article_Display_Page/0,,PTID236518_CHID438620_CIID1031864,00.html.

[vii] Solomon, Barbara. "Growing Up, Acting Out." Parents. June 11, 2015. http://www.parents.com/parenting/better-parenting/teenagers/growing-up-acting-out/.

[viii] Merriam-Webster OnLine, s.v. "father," accessed November 17, 2012, http://www.merriam- webster.com/dictionary/father.

[ix] "The American family today." Pew Research Center's Social & Demographic Trends Project. December 17, 2015. http://www.pewsocialtrends.org/2015/12/17/1-the-american-family-today/.

[x] "Marriage, Family, & Stepfamily Statistics." Smart Stepfamilies. April 2014. http://www.smartstepfamilies.com/view/statistics.

[xi] National Fatherhood Initiative, accessed November 05, 2012, http://www.fatherhood.org.

[xii] "Employment status of the civilian population by race, sex, and age," United States Department of Labor, accessed October 2012, http://www.bls.gov/news.release/empsit.t02.htm.

[xiii] Whitehead, Barbara. *Opposing Viewpoints.* San Diego: Greenhaven Press, 1993.

[xiv] Watch D.O.G.S., accessed November 07, 2012, http://www.fathers.com.

[xv] "Children in single-parent families by race," National Kids Count Program, accessed November 17, 2012, http://datacenter.kidscount.org/data/tables/107-children-in-single-parent-families-by-race#detailed/1/any/false/869,36,868,867,133/10,11,9,12,1,185,13/432,431.

[xvi] "Single Motherhood in the United States – A Snapshot (2012)," The Women's Legal Defense and Education Fund, accessed November 10, 2012, https://www.legalmomentum.org/sites/default/files/reports/single-mothers-snapshot_0.pdf.

[xvii] "Criminal Justice Fact Sheet," NAACP, accessed November 5, 2012, http://www.naacp.org/pages/criminal-justice-fact-sheet.

[xviii] Quigley, Bill. "40 Reasons Why Our Jails Are Full of Black and Poor People." The Huffington Post. June 02, 2015. http://www.huffingtonpost.com/bill-quigley/40-reasons-why-our-jails-are-full-of-black-and-poor-people_b_7492902.html.

[xix] "Criminal Justice Fact Sheet." NAACP. http://www.naacp.org/criminal-justice-fact-sheet/.

[xx] The Institute for Responsible Fatherhood and Family Revitalization, accessed November 1, 2012, http://www.responsiblefatherhood.org.

[xxi] Real Dads Network, accessed November 02, 2012, http://realdadsnetwork.org/.

[xxii] The Real M.E.N.S. Project, accessed November 10, 2012, http://www.realmensproject.org/ (site discontinued).

[xxiii] *REAL DAD Magazine*, accessed November 03, 2012, http://www.realdadmagazine.com.

[xxiv] National Fatherhood Initiative, accessed November 05, 2012, http://www.fatherhood.org/mission-and-values.

[xxv] "What Do We Know About Social and Emotional Development in Early Childhood?" The Urban Child Institute. http://www.urbanchildinstitute.org/resources/publications/good-start/social-and-emotional-development.

[xxvi] Michigan Department of Community Health. "Social-Emotional Development in Young Children." Michigan.gov. December 2003. https://www.michigan.gov/documents/Social_Emotional_Development_in_Young_Children_Guide_88553_7.pdf.

[xxvii] "The Importance of Fathers in the Healthy Development of Children," Child Welfare Information Gateway, accessed April 6, 2016, https://www.childwelfare.gov/pubs/usermanuals/fatherhood/.

[xxviii] Child Trends. https://www.childtrends.org.

[xxix] Bonczar, Thomas P. "Prevalence of Imprisonment in the US Population, 1974-2001." Bureau of Justice Statistics. August 2003. https://www.bis.gov/content/pub/pdf/piusp01/pdf.

[xxx] The American Civil Liberties Union, and The Rights Working Group. "The Persistence of Racial and Ethnic Profiling in the United States." ACLU. June 30, 2009.

[xxxi] Sayers, Shoshannah. "Mass Incarceration & People of Color." Southern Coalition for Social Justice. April 15, 2014. http://www.southerncoaltion.org/mass-incarceration-people-color/

[xxxii] Wilf, Rachel. "Disparities in School Discipline Move Students of Color Toward Prison." Center for American Progress. March 13, 2012. https://www.americanprogress.org/issues/race/news/2012/03/13/11350/disparities-in-school-discipline-move-students-of-color-toward-prison/.

[xxxiii] Rabury,Bernadette, and Daniel Kopf. "Prisons of Poverty: Uncovering the Pre-incarceration incomes of the imprisoned." Prison Policy initiative. July 9, 2015. https://www.prisonpolicy.org/reports/income.html.

[xxxiv] Munroe, Myles. Unlealsh Your Purpose. Shippensburg:Destiny Image, Inc., 2011.

[xxxv] Alexander, Michelle. "More Black Men Are In Prison Today Than Were Enslaved In 1850." The Huffington Post. October 12, 2011. http://www.huffingtonpost.com/2011/10/12/michelle-alexander-more-black-men-in-prison-slaves-1850_n_1007368.html.

[xxxvi] "Young Adults in Jail or Prison." Child Trends. April 2012. https://www.childtrends.org/indicators/young-adults-in-jail-or-prison/.

[xxxvii] Kerby, Sophia. "The Top 10 Most Startling Facts About People of Color and Criminal Justice in the United States." Center for American Progress. May 29, 2015. https://www.americanprogress.org/issues/race/news/2012/03/13/11351/the-top-10-most-startling-facts-about-people-of-color-and-criminal-justice-in-the-united-states/.

[xxxviii] Gregoire, Carolyn. "Dropout Rates: Student Journalist Investigates High School Dropout Crisis (VIDEO)." The Huffington Post. January 30, 2012. http://www.huffingtonpost.com/2012/01/30/dropout-rates_n_1241959.html.

[xxxix] America's Promise Alliance. "High School Graduation Rates Rise in Some Major U.S. Cities, But Significant Work Remains to Curb Dropout Crisis." PR Newswire. April 21, 2009. http://www.prnewswire.com/news-releases/high-school-graduation-rates-rise-in-some-major-us-cities-but-significant-work-remains-to-curb-dropout-crisis-61901157.html.

[xl] "American Cancer Society Recommendations for Prostate Cancer Early Detection." American Cancer Society. https://www.cancer.org/cancer/prostate-cancer/early-detection/acs-recommendations.html.

[xli] "Key Statistics for Prostate Cancer | Prostate Cancer Facts." American Cancer Society. https://www.cancer.org/cancer/prostate-cancer/about/key-statistics.html.

[xlii] Gordon, Marcy. "FDIC: 21.4 percent of black families don't have bank accounts." TheGrio. September 12, 2012. http://thegrio.com/2012/09/12/fdic-21-4-percent-of-black-families-dont-have-bank-accounts/.

[xliii] Stankich, Brian Daniel. "How Much Money Does the Average American Family Have in Savings?" Synonym. March 31, 2017. http://classroom.synonym.com/much-money-average-american-family-savings-17261.html.

[xliv] Huddleston, Cameron. "69% of Americans Have Less Than $1,000 in Savings." GOBankingRates. September 19, 2016. https://www.gobankingrates.com/personal-finance/data-americans-savings/.

[xlv] "Growing Older in America: The Health and Retirement Study." National Institute on Aging. September 02, 2011. https://www.nia.nih.gov/health/publication/growing-older-america-health-and-retirement-study/chapter-2-work-and-retirement.

[xlvi] "Questions and Answers about Military Families: A Sloan Work and Family Research Network Fact Sheet." Sloan Work and Family Research Network. February 2009. https://workfamily.sas.upenn.edu/sites/workfamily.sas.upenn.edu/files/imported/pdfs/militaryfamilies.pdf.

[xlvii] "Veterans Survey." Pew Research Center's Social & Demographic Trends Project. November 27, 2012. http://www.pewsocialtrends.org/2012/11/27/the-veterans-survey/.

www.ingramcontent.com/pod-product-compliance
Ingram Content Group UK Ltd.
Pitfield, Milton Keynes, MK11 3LW, UK
UKHW061430110926
15112UKWH00025B/219

9 781962 110655